POOR KNOW MORE

i

POOR KNOW MORE

~~~~~~~~~~~~~~~~~~~~~~~~~~~~~~~~~~~

An Inspiring Journey to Financial Peace

~~~~~~~~~~~~~~~~~~~~~~~~~~~~~~~~~~~

DOREEN VAIL

Foreword by Kelvin Boston

DEDICATION

I dedicate this book to God first!
It was all Your idea. I just did as I was instructed.

I also dedicate this book to my husband and best friend, Seth.
There is no way that I could have ever done this without you.

And to my daughters, Crystale and Taryn.
Your photography and editing skills are priceless.

This was definitely a family affair.

TABLE OF CONTENTS

FOREWORD

by Kelvin E. Boston

Poor Know More explores how the Moneywise Empowerment Tour has helped thousands of attendees eliminate their fear of being poor (financially, emotionally, or spiritually) because they left the conference knowing more about the wealth-building process.

Poor Know More is Doreen Vail's interpretation of my expression "Poor No More", which helps explain the mission of the Moneywise Empowerment Tour. The Tour is a traveling community-based financial conference. It empowers attendees with financial information and helps them understand that if they know more, then they can stop worrying about being poor.

People from all walks of life attend the Moneywise Tour. Some are financially secure, and some have never felt financially secure in their life. Still, in spite of their economic circumstances, they all wanted to know more about managing their finances, building wealth, or successfully operating a business. Like most Americans, many of them needed this information because no one had ever taught them how to manage their financial affairs in a manner that would help them live poor no more.

John Bryant, Founder and CEO of Operation Hope, is a Moneywise Tour speaker. During his Moneywise talk, he explained that "being broke is a temporary financial situation but being poor can be a debilitating state of mind." To succeed financially in life, John says, "you must decide never to be poor."

Today, 43 million Americans live in poverty. People of color have the highest rates of poverty in the U.S. What is most alarming is the fact that many middle-income American households are just one paycheck or medical emergency away from poverty. American households that have been able to accumulate a few assets must often use their savings to help other less fortunate family members. So, in the end, most American households can be affected by poverty's ability to debilitate a person's financial, emotional, or spiritual well-being. This is why Doreen's book is so timely and needed.

Americans from all walks of life need to understand that the key to being poor no more is to know more. We all need to know how to succeed in a capitalistic society. It is not easy to do so. It is assumed that because you live in the USA, you understand how to *succeed* in the USA. However, we do not. There are no classes that teach success in America. We must all figure it out for ourselves, the best way we can.

Some Americans have learned how to successfully play the great financial game of life. But far too many Americans never learn the rules of the game. The Moneywise Empowerment Tour teaches people how to play successfully. Doreen's book shares how the Moneywise Tour helped her play this wealth-building game. She learned that to win this game, you must know the rules of the game and be willing to play it.

In this book, she also shares the various strategies that the Moneywise Tour's thought leaders, speakers, and presenters use to become masterful at wealth-building. In doing so, she shows how knowing more about the great financial game of life will keep you from being poor in spirit and finances.

When I asked Doreen to join the Moneywise Tour, I had no idea that she would become the crown jewel of the tour. I knew she was a great vocalist. But she is so much more. She is also a great speaker, motivator, and leader. I didn't know that she had a story to tell our audience or that people would always want to hear more from that small woman who had the amazing voice. I didn't know the power she would have on the Moneywise audiences. Now I know. I also know that Doreen is a great motivational thought leader as well. She can and has stood shoulder to shoulder with the men and women she respectfully writes about in this book. While on the Moneywise tour, she has inspired thousands of people from every part of the country.

Doreen has learned a lot from attending the Moneywise conferences over the years. She is probably our best student. She has always been eager to share what she learned with others. Now she has compiled many of her Moneywise "know more" moments in this book. She could have kept her newfound financial wisdom to herself. But that is not her way. Knowing more about financial success has helped Doreen understand that she is "poor no more." Now she wants you to have the same opportunity and experience. Enjoy this book and understand that you will be poor no more because you will know more about the great financial game of life.

Kelvin Boston, CEO
Moneywise TV Network

Introduction

A RESET OF A MINDSET

"The second sky is a place above the clouds in your life.
The second sky is a place where you can see the sunlight.
The second sky is above all of the cares and the strife.
The second sky is a new direction in your life."

I was never one to be frivolous with money. I grew up hearing, "Cut those lights off when you leave the room!" and "Close that refrigerator door! You're letting all the cold air out!" I definitely knew what it was like to shop in the clearance section and I did not own my one and only designer bag until my daughter was old enough to purchase one for me. For what seemed to be most of my life, there was always some kind of financial catastrophe that I was either going into, in the midst of, or coming out of. I had no financial peace, which affected other areas of my life, and I was not traveling this road alone. It seemed like many people in my family, at my job, in my church, and in my neighborhood were experiencing similar challenges. We all talked about or listened to one another's financial woes. However, being in the same boat without the wisdom of a captain, we drifted from one financial crisis to another with no lasting resolution. It would become an expectation and a mindset that this was just the way of life for working class people like us. We didn't know any other way and we didn't know any better. We had a hope but no plan; a desire but no knowledge. Our wisdom only went as far as the wisest person in our circle at the time and I was sometimes that person. My world stayed pretty much status quo until I found myself in the company of people who had a wealth of financial knowledge and wisdom that they wanted to share.

It was at a benefit concert where, unbeknownst to me, a multimillionaire sat in the audience enjoying my performance. He later came to my table, purchased a CD, introduced himself, and spoke briefly with my husband and me. I did not know at the time that he would be instrumental in helping me change my entire financial outlook on life. I soon found myself experiencing the opportunity of a lifetime through traveling the country with an elite group of enlightened wealthy men and women. The more I traveled, the more comfortable I became with the company that I was now keeping. To my surprise, many of them were just as amazed at my singing as I was at their speaking! I could not believe that the world did not know about these incredible people. However, I would soon learn that some of the world *did* know about them, it was *my* world that did not know. It was at this point that I discovered my purpose for being on this tour. I was having v a reset of my mindset and my assignment was to tell *my* part of the world what I was learning from my exposure to the world of enlightened and wealthy multimillionaires.

We are so influenced today by the lifestyles of the rich and famous that we watch on television. However, what is portrayed as reality on TV is not every wealthy person's reality. There are some common traits and habits that make and keep people wealthy. There are also some common traits and habits that make and keep people poor. I needed to know more of what wealthy people knew and put that knowledge into practice if I was to be poor no more. My part of the world needed the knowledge of experienced captains for our financial ships in order to say goodbye to our financial hardships. I was afforded this rare opportunity of being in the presence of wealthy, enlightened, and humble individuals as they taught on stage and conversed over dinner. I learned that it is not the amount of money alone that establishes one's potential for wealth, but it is indeed a mindset and a lifestyle. I was in the early stages of a reset of my mindset and beginning my journey to financial peace. My definition of wealth was about to change drastically. I knew that one day, I was to share everything that I learned. So here I am, writing my first book, *Poor Know More*, for you. Come travel this wonderful journey of a life filled with wealth, abundance, and peace with me. The more you know, the more you can say, "No more!"

Know more:

- *Wealth takes a reset of your mindset followed by a change in your behavior.*
- *Change happens one thought at a time.*
- *Wealth gives you the power to have more choices.*

Lesson 1

MY HOMESCHOOL COURSE ON FINANCES

"While my mind is trying to understand all the hurt and pain,
Is it in God's plan?
My heart knows what my mind can't conceive."

I was born in Brooklyn, New York. However, I have no memories of living in our two-bedroom apartment. When I was just a little over 2 years old, my parents moved from the Fort Greene housing projects to Hempstead, Long Island. My mother said that my father did not want to buy a home, but she was adamant about not raising her children in the projects. I remember our new home being massive to me! It was a big white house with five bedrooms, two full bathrooms, a formal living room, a finished basement, and a detached 2-car garage! The backyard was like our very own park with swings and enough green grass to play endless games of dodgeball and softball. It was like a dream to me. I remember laying in the grass in the middle of our yard daydreaming as I watched the clouds go by. I had no idea how much our small piece of heaven cost or what it took to make such a large leap from the projects to home ownership. But what I *did* know is that our family of six (later seven) lived on the "Island" in a great house that all our relatives from the city loved to visit. George Jefferson had nothing on the way the Hardys had moved on up!

My mother enjoyed having nice things and wanted her family to have and look their best. She had beautiful furniture covered in plastic in a beautiful living room that we were never allowed to sit in. There was lovely new furniture in my parents' bedroom and as time went on, all the children would get new furniture, too. She chose to charge some of the things that she wanted for herself and the family (the "buy now, pay later" plan). It was very important for her family to look good on the outside at all costs and she worked hard to make that happen. We were always dressed very nicely, no matter if our clothes were paid for at full price, on clearance, handmade by my grandmother, or free when my father would bring boxes of donated clothing home. My mother, my two older sisters, and I also went to the beautician every two weeks to get our hair done. As a matter of fact, the mother of the great and legendary basketball player Julius Erving, aka Dr. J, was our beautician. I thought she was an amazing lady. I was always impressed at how Mrs. Lindsay could talk, watch her soap opera on the little black-and-white television, and straighten my hair all at the same time. I always left her shop feeling so pretty. I'll never forget the day that Julius came into the shop to visit his mom. My head was back in the sink being washed and all I could see was from his chest up. He was very tall, handsome, and had a very big afro. It seemed that not long afterwards, I remember my mother talking about how Mrs. Lindsay would not be doing hair anymore if her son signed some contract. As time went on, my mother later said that Mrs. Lindsay would not be working a job ever again. Aside from losing a great beautician whom I adored and would not nick my ears with the hot comb, all that talk went right over my head. However, in my later years, I understood the honor of seeing Julius Erving and the honor of being a client of his precious mother. He kept his promise and I was so sad for us when we had to find a new beautician. I must admit that no one else has ever measured up to my Mrs. Lindsay.

Although a lot of money and time was put into the appearance of our home, it came at a cost. We were latchkey kids because my mother had a day job and a night job. I clearly remember those rare days when, as I approached our house while walking home from school, I could see my bedroom window open with the curtains flying through it. That was the amazing signal to me that my mother was home and had cooked dinner and cleaned my room. The most beautiful memory I have are those times when I opened the door to the smell of food, open windows, and my mother being there. However, those "Leave It to Beaver" moments would dissipate towards the end of the month when tension would rise in our home between my parents. My mother's countenance would change, and she appeared worried and unhappy. Her patience would also run very short with her children during those times. Although just a child, I had begun to figure out the cycle and some of the things that would make my mother unhappy. In time, I learned to hate these people named "LILCO" and "Mortgage" who seemed to cause my mother such dismay every month. She would say things like, "LILCO is taking all my money!" or "All I am doing is working to pay LILCO!" It would be years before I would find out that LILCO stood for the Long Island Lighting Company. At the time, I just didn't know why we were yelled at for leaving lights on or the refrigerator door open too long. As children, we had no idea that energy cost anything, especially a lot of money. I also wondered what a mortgage was. I thought they paid for the house when they bought it. My understanding of buying something at that age was that you did not get what you wanted until after you paid for it. Or you could put the item on layaway, which meant that it stayed in the store until it was all paid for. This was the beginning of my homeschooling in finance. I had no idea that I was being taught life-long lessons and I am sure that my parents had no idea what they were teaching their children about finances. However, even from the eyes of a child, these lessons in finance definitely had some holes in it.

I was also taught a lot about finances by watching my father. He was an entrepreneur who dreamed big and spent big. His pockets always seemed to be filled with money. I never quite understood my mother's complaint about not having money when it appeared that my father always had plenty to have fun with. He seemed to always have enough to eat out, go bowling, dress very nicely, and have great parties in our home. He was always working on the cars that filled our garage and driveway. He also did home improvement jobs for clients. I would sometimes overhear people comment about how great my father was working with his hands. However, sometimes the following comment would be that he seldom finishes the job. I do not recall him working a regular 9-to-5 job for very long. Instead, my father had an entrepreneurial spirit. He owned several businesses. The ones that I remember most are the laundromat, hardware store, and restaurant. All his children were his employees. He owned the laundromat the longest and we worked before and after school and all day during our summer vacations. We washed, dried, and folded more loads of clothing than I can count to this day. The laundromat was the only one in town to have a pick-up and delivery service. It was before the invention of disposable diapers and we washed loads and loads of dirty diapers. We rarely got paid except for getting dimes out of the coin-operated dryers to buy candy. During this homeschool lesson, I learned to work for free! My mother was his full-time employee at the laundromat, but she would also work another full-time job. I now realize that our dream home probably would have slipped away from us long before it actually did if my mother had not worked the other jobs. My father had big dreams for all his businesses and we all got on his train of hope and enthusiasm over the potential of being rich. As children, we would watch him empty all the machines and take what appeared to us to be thousands of dollars in coins out of the door. Yet at home, the lack of money constantly seemed to be the cause of so many arguments between my parents. I just never understood how we could be so rich and yet so poor. However, my father's philosophy relating to finances seemed to be to carry your cash on you and spend it on what you want first, then pay your bills last and save nothing. Knowing what I now know, I realize that my father had the potential to accomplish his goals. What he lacked was the knowledge needed to be a great businessman, and a reset of his mindset from one of a poor mentality to practicing wealthy strategies. Perhaps a greater understanding of the power of partnerships would have helped also. However, this would have been a challenging task because ✓ taking advice and trusting people were sensitive issues for him. So, he would continue to make the same mistakes. My father had the skills and the talent to be successful, but as I would later learn, you need more than that to succeed. We all worked hard as a family for the dream, but all the businesses failed after having just a measure of success. However, there were many, many lessons taught and learned for the good and the not-so-good.

✓ A visual lesson that had a significant impact on my homeschooling occurred one night after my father had fallen asleep. I saw my mother crawling on the floor and quietly dragging his pants out of their bedroom. She looked up at me and placed her finger over her lips, instructing me to be quiet as she dragged his pants into the next room. She removed and counted the money that filled his pockets. She kept some of it and put the rest back into the pockets before returning his pants to their original place. I thought it strange and could not stop staring at what was happening. Was it stealing or not? Does my father know, or should I tell him? I was a child trying to process adult financial interactions. I had often heard my mother ask my father for money and his answer would be that he didn't have any. I later learned that this was her way of getting money from him to pay the bills before he spent it. Evidently, expecting my father to give her the money was not the behavior model between the two of them. That lesson stayed in my psyche into adulthood and although my husband says it never happened, I must admit that after we were married, I once dragged my husband's pants out of the bedroom to go through his pockets for money. I had to explain to my husband that the entire act hinged on him not knowing. At the time, I was doing what I had learned and seen as a child and what I thought I had to do. But I never had to ask my husband to contribute to the household for anything because I had complete control of our finances. I am happy to report that although we made many financial mistakes, that learned behavior was never practiced again in our home. The financial model that we developed for the home we made together was built on maturity and trust.

My first lesson and interaction with a bill collector was when I was in elementary school. I must have been somewhere between the ages of nine and ten years old. I answered the phone one night while my mother was at work. When I told the man on the phone that my parents were not at home, he proceeded to tell me that "little girls who lie go to hell!" I remember his words like I just got the call yesterday. He also stated that my parents could go to jail if they did not call him back that night! I was terrified! Not only was I going to become a foster child, but he said I was also going to hell! Now this was way before consumer protection laws were put into place. Back then, bill collectors could absolutely terrorize you at your job and at all hours of the day and night. When my mother came home, I was so afraid to tell her about the call, but I could not hold back. My mother wanted the exact words that the man had said to me and the only thing scarier than going to hell was to say the word "hell" to my mother. By the time I finally got it out, I was a crying mess and my mother was furious! As they did back then, she sent me out of the room before making the return call and it was for my own good, I'm sure. I learned a great lesson that night through my interactions with the bill collector and my mother. My take away from the experience was to avoid those nasty bill collection calls at all costs. As an adult in debt and behind in payments, I would think to myself, "Just don't answer the phone," and then hope that they would stop calling. Of course, the end result for that practice was not beneficial for me or my family. I would later learn that bills don't go, they grow!

It was my paternal grandmother Nana who, after coming from North Carolina to live with us in New York, taught us the lesson of saving. She walked me downtown to her bank when I was a little girl and opened my first savings account. I remember going up to the teller's window with my little bank book to deposit small amounts of money into my account. The bank had an aroma that was different from anything I had ever smelled. I loved keeping up with how much money I was saving. I was so proud of that book that had my signature on it. I had dreams of seeing my money grow and grow because Nana said that would happen if I just left it in the bank. Sadly however, since saving was not emphasized in our household and spending was, my savings account was very short-lived. I don't remember when or what the money was spent on. It was just gone. The reality is that this is probably the shortest homeschool lesson on finances that I was given.

I did not learn how my parents lost our beautiful home on Long Island until many decades later. During a conversation with my now elderly mother, I learned that fifteen years into a twenty-year mortgage, the beautiful home that we cherished so much was sold for one dollar plus back taxes. The mortgage that I did not understand as a child was $128 a month. I was a teenager at the time we lost the house and all I knew was that we no longer owned our home on the "Island." It was gone, just like the one and only new car that I ever remember my mother owning. No explanation was ever given at the time. Little did I know what lay ahead for me in my adult life. It would be decades later, while on the <u>Moneywise Empowerment Tour</u> and dining with <u>millionaires,</u> that I would realize that the opportunities that my parents had to be wealthy were many. My parents just needed to know more so that they could say "no more" to dreams lost and overwhelming debt. They needed an action plan and a balanced partnership. My father had a dream and great talent, but he didn't have a plan or a good work ethic. My mother had a great work ethic but didn't have a dream that she believed enough in. My parents just did not know. Or perhaps they knew more than I think they knew and just did not put it into practice. However, the most awesome thing to come out of all of this is hearing my 80+ year old mother get excited about her life and her finances as I shared with her what I have learned while being a part of the Moneywise Empowerment Tour! The roles have reversed, and she says that she has learned more from me about finances than she has ever known. She told me that she really did not know how to conduct her finances because she had never been taught properly. She stated that she had no idea what a bill was until after she was married. The remarkable thing about life is that it's never too late to learn, know, change, and grow!

Today, I understand the <u>financial errors that my parents made,</u> but not before I made a boatload of my own mistakes. I definitely put into practice the lessons that I had learned at home. The main ones were that money was meant to be carried in your pockets and displayed on your back and in your home, that it may be used as a tool during a power struggle, and that you earned money to spend money. I learned to live beyond what I could afford, to ignore my bills until they became a problem, to work more jobs, and to hold on at all costs to what I had accumulated. Most of all, I learned that money destroys relationships. However, through my interactions with financially sound individuals, some considered wealthy and some not, I had a reset of my mindset. I wanted to change some of my behaviors. My new education taught me that many wealthy people carry little-to-no cash in their pockets. Some do not display their wealth through what they have on or where they live. They make credit work for them and use it wisely. I was taught how to play the credit score game of keeping low to zero balances and making payments before the 30-day grace period. They instructed me how to form valuable and trustworthy partnerships to reach financial goals together. They save, invest, give, and spend their money almost in that order. I was also taught that financial mistakes are inevitable, but it is important to address and correct them quickly. The wealthy also use money to leverage power and not just as consumers of goods and services. Lastly, I was taught that they learn from their mistakes and know that there is always the opportunity to start over again.

We must understand that children are learning life-long financial habits from the behaviors that they see in their homes. There is always a class in session on finances and the adults are the instructors with no days off. Every shopping trip, pay period, vacation, trip to the bank, child support payment, credit card purchase, dinner out, penny jar, piggy bank, savings account, new car purchase, new home purchase, Christmas, birthday, and bill that comes in the mail can be a financially teachable moment. When our girls were in elementary school and we used to go out for family dinners, we would play a game in which we saw who could come closest to guessing the entire bill amount. It was a very teachable moment of how much eating out cost our family. I would also let them read the receipt after grocery shopping so that they understood how much everything that they wanted in the grocery store cost. It's what you do with those little teachable moments that may help your children grow into financially stable adults. People pay hundreds of dollars to go to seminars to learn how to financially empower themselves as adults and undo the free financial education that they had growing up during their homeschool education.

Know more:

- *The home is one of the greatest classrooms that a child will ever sit in when it comes to financial education.*
- *Children are taught to be wealthy. Children are taught to be poor.*
- *It's not the size of your house, it's the size of the heart in your home.*
- *You must understand how past life lessons affect your present actions.*
- *The eyes of a child are always watching, and their minds are always learning.*

14

Lesson 2

THE BANKRUPTCY LESSON

"All I know is I'm gonna fly again.

It's just gonna take some time for my wounds to heal.

It won't be easy, but I know I'll spread my wings.

And it won't be long, I'll be in the air real soon."

I was sitting in the court house parking lot writing in my journal and repeatedly asking God, "How did I get here?" It was a beautiful but hot summer day and although there was not a cloud in the sky, there was plenty of water falling. The tears that were rolling down my face would not stop coming. It was time for my day in court. My husband had already filed Chapter 13 bankruptcy and had his time in front of the judge. However, I had prayed so hard that my day would never come. I was hoping that by some miraculous turn of events, all our bills and all the creditors would somehow just disappear. I wanted to avoid this great humiliation and admission of being a failure in front of a judge and other strangers. But there would be no miracle for me that day. It was time for me to go face my greatest fear.

Months earlier, our credit counselor told us that our finances were "hemorrhaging" and that there was only one option for us. Even when he suggested that we file for bankruptcy, my husband and I both knew that was something that we absolutely did not want to do! Our response was, "But that's what deadbeats do to get out of paying their debt! We want to pay the people that we owed. Just tell us how we can do it." We had purchased the items or services and we planned to pay for them, no matter how long it might take us. However, our bankruptcy lawyer explained to us that our options were few and bankruptcy was the best and almost the only way for us to avoid losing everything. He explained that filing would save our home from foreclosure and give us some relief from the extreme pressure that we were under. At this time, we were either unemployed or under-employed, having taken big pay cuts. So, with hesitation and much regret, we agreed to file and take the seven-year hit to our credit. It had taken us a long time of diligence and hard work to build up our credit and it was about to have an ugly stain on it that would take seven years to remove. I was devastated!

This was my greatest financial traumatic event. To say that I felt like such a failure while sitting in that hot car on the courthouse grounds is an understatement. I never personally knew anyone who had filed for bankruptcy. There was no one that I could talk to about this. I thought that we would never recover from the black stain on our credit report. Also, I felt that people would look down on us if they knew. For me, it was a big ugly secret that had to be kept from everyone, especially our children, friends, and family. No one knew that we were in such dire straits financially. We were able to put on a really good face for the world. No one had any idea of the duress we were under and the sleepless nights we endured. I knew the toll that financial trauma had taken on people lives. I had seen people crying and couples arguing in the bankruptcy attorney's office. All these thoughts were going through my head as I sat in my car and cried. I wrote all my feelings down in my journal until it was time to go in and have my day in court. I also wrote my emotions down because this was my way of talking to God and I never wanted to forget the trauma of that day. I documented all the guilt, shame, and hopelessness that I was feeling at the time. Not only was I bankrupt in my finances, but my spirit felt bankrupt, too!

I waited until the absolute last minute before exiting my car and entering the courthouse. The fear and anxiety of someone I knew seeing me there was almost paralyzing! As I opened the door to the waiting area for the bankruptcy hearings, I was taken aback by who and what I saw! There were people of all nationalities, cultures, and occupations. There were people in varying styles of dress, from jeans to business attire. There were people both young and old and everything in between. The room was packed with all kinds of people! As I stood there amazed at what I saw, I understood the one common denominator that we all shared. We were all in trouble with our finances. The journey that each of us took to get there were as different as the people standing in that crowded room. However, on that day, we were all there seeking relief from our financial burden. As for me, it was my last and very shameful resort. In my mind, bankruptcy equated to failure. I found myself once again asking the same question, "What am I doing here?" It was then that I heard with extreme clarity, "You are here because of them. This is your ministry to help others get through the pain and shame that you are feeling right now."

Now I must be honest when I say that I did not understand, see, or even feel how I would ever be able to help someone else, given my present situation. I wanted this day to be over and to get as far away from the shame and pain as I could. At that time, I did not know that within a few short years, I would find myself singing and speaking in front of audiences about my financial journey. It was when I least expected it or even wanted to talk about it that I would feel the need to share the story of my financial struggles. To my dismay, that feeling would often come during the times when the audience seemed to be celebrating me and my performance the most. But I soon realized that those times when I was held to such high esteem were the perfect times to share my journey. Someone needed to know that I used to be right where they are now. After sharing my bankruptcy story, without fail, there was always someone who wanted to share their story with me. I often found myself counseling, encouraging, and praying for individuals and couples who waited to speak to me at the end of the event. I cannot count how many heads were hung in shame or how many tears were cried on my shoulder or how many times I told married couples not to allow their finances to destroy their marriage. I was now that person, the one that I needed to talk to back when I was sitting in tears in that hot car outside the courthouse. I listened, I comforted, and I encouraged to the best of my ability. There were so many people who told me how much better they felt just hearing that someone else had navigated the same waters they felt they were drowning in and not just survived but thrived.

Although statistically, more marriages end because of finances than any other reason, my husband and I are living examples that a marriage can sustain extreme financial hardship and survive. Actually, a marriage can thrive *through* financial hardship. We both made a conscientious choice not to allow hardships and financial trauma to ruin our marriage. We got into this mess together and we worked through it together. We became accountable to one another financially. We attended financial education classes together. We worked on rebuilding our credit together and even made it fun. We discovered new and exciting ways to enjoy life and still live within our means. Most of all, we forgave ourselves and said goodbye to the guilt and shame. Working through our struggles strengthened our relationship. But it took a real mature commitment from both of us. We attended a workshop for people who have experienced bankruptcy and followed through on what we were taught. Over time, our damaged credit rating was not only restored but eventually surpassed our previous credit scores! But it took a great amount of patience and diligence. We learned that we could change bad habits and also work through hard times without going under. We had a reset of our mindset. We went on to purchase more cars and homes with lower interest rates than before filing bankruptcy. We did not only achieve restoration, we exceeded what we had previously achieved. It was a long walk but we did it together. So now I want to speak to that couple who are in the grips of financial hopelessness and shame. To you I say, don't give up! The road is long and hard, but you can get through this together. Rebuilding is hard and tedious work, but the payout is life-altering. Make your path to financial recovery unusual and fun. No extra money for eating out for a special occasion? My husband once set up our living room like a restaurant for our anniversary when we couldn't afford to eat out. He took our round glass table out of the kitchen and set it up in the living room. He printed menus using the computer for the Chinese food that he had ordered. My husband then had my youngest daughter act as the waitress, taking our orders as our oldest daughter played her violin in the background. Both our girls were in elementary school and they giggled with joy the entire time. They ran up the steps and disappeared to give us time alone. It was one of the best and most memorable celebrations I have ever had! The lessons we learned through this journey helped solidify our marriage. It made our bond stronger, not weaker. As of today, we have been married for over forty years and still counting! We would have missed out on all these wonderful years, had we thrown in the towel decades ago.

I wrote this chapter because of what I experienced in bankruptcy court. Although I did not know it then, I went through all that to get to this point in my life. I am here to encourage, motivate, and inspire others to get through their financial trauma. Bankruptcy is not an option to be taken lightly, but it is a viable and a legal option to get relief from insurmountable debt and a fresh start. Bankruptcy is a new beginning, not an ending. You can overcome financial trauma. Not only can you recover from it but you can discover financial freedom and peace of mind. Start by forgiving yourself. When you know more, you can say, "No more!"

Know more:

- *Sometimes never giving up means letting go.*
- *Failure can be a door to greater opportunities.*
- *Go beyond recovering from financial trauma to discovering financial peace.*
- *Forgive yourself for past financial mistakes.*

Lesson 3

THE ROUND GLASS TABLE

"When my mind says there's no money to pay all the bills,
My heart says stand on His promises.
God can, and He will.
My heart knows what my mind can't conceive."

It was 3:00 am and I sat with my face in my hands and my elbows resting on the round glass table with the chrome metal base. The tears were running down my face and I was feeling hopeless. I had searched so long for this table that fit perfectly in the bay window of our kitchen. This was the first home that my husband and I had ever purchased, and we watched it being built from the ground up! We chose the location, the style, every appliance, and all the flooring that went into our brand-new house. The bay window that I insisted on having allowed so much light into our townhouse and I loved sitting at that table, feeling the warmth of the sun. I had watched our girls play in the snow, play games with their friends, trick or treat, and later, park their cars, all from sitting at that table. All the visitors to our home seemed to crowd around that glass table, which sat only four people, for good food and great conversation. However, at that moment, in the wee hours of the night, there was no sun, no warmth, no family or friends, and no pleasure in sitting at that table.

Instead of holding delicious food, the round glass table was now covered with white envelopes containing our household bills. My eyes were burning, and I was exhausted to the point of wanting to give up. I had gone through the bills multiple times and even if we paid the minimum due, we still did not have enough money from our paychecks to pay them all. My husband and I had already been through a total of four bankruptcies between the two of us. We were trying to save our home from foreclosure and had filed enough "chapters" to write a book! Although the bankruptcies took some of the pressure from our creditors off, money was still very, very tight! We were still drowning in student loans, car payments, and keeping up with the new mortgage arrangement. I had a career as an Occupational Therapy Assistant and my husband was an engineer for a government contracting company. However, we had both taken big pay cuts due to layoffs and decreased working hours. As if that were not enough to deal with, I was really feeling the pull on my heart and my life to pursue music as a ministry and a career. So, at 3:00 am, I sat at a table that had served so many loving meals and was the main gathering place in our home. However, that same table was now a place of great pain, hopelessness, and sorrow. Our dream home had turned into a nightmare. We were poor, and I didn't know what to do. I felt like I was drowning. With tears flowing, it was at that moment that I began to talk to and to hear from God. It was also at that moment that I would begin my journey into being poor no more and discovering financial peace.

The great author and speaker Maya Angelou is quoted as saying, *"Do the best you can until you know better. Then when you know better, do better."* However, at that point, my question was, "How do I increase my knowledge so that I will know how to do better in my finances?" I felt so lost that I did not know enough to even ask the right questions. Who in my circle had the knowledge that I needed? My parents' homeschooling on finances was a recipe for how to struggle and live paycheck to paycheck. Business and finances were not taught in any of my courses in public school or college. I had spent my entire financial life just trying to keep my head above water but making the same mistakes over and over again. I was aware that there were very wealthy people in the world, but I thought that they were either born into it or had hit some sort of lottery or stroke of good luck. My religious upbringing taught me about suffering and giving but not so much about what to do after I finished praying for a miracle. I didn't think that there was any rhyme or reason as to why some people were wealthy and others were not. I did not know that the possibility was open to all of us. I also didn't know that we are taught how to be poor or how to be wealthy. It would be much later in my life that I would discover that there is a common knowledge that wealthy people have and share among themselves which the average person does not often have access to. However, at that moment, while sitting at the glass table in the wee hours of the morning, while everyone else was asleep, I knew we needed help! I needed a divine intervention.

With tears rolling down my face, I sincerely prayed and asked God for precise instructions on how to get out of this pit and prison of debt. Every part of me was exhausted and I felt hopeless. I laid my head down on the cold glass. It was then that I heard a voice audibly speaking to my heart that asked me, "What do you want?" I did not know if it was fatigue, if I was just hearing things, or if I had fallen asleep. But I responded and said, "To be able to pay all our bills this month." Then I heard the same question again, "What do you want?" Thinking that my first response was not enough, my second response was, "Okay, to pay all the bills and to have enough money left over for groceries and gas." I heard the same question asked a third time. This time I decided to ask for what I wanted and not just what I thought I could have. My third and final response was, "To pay all our bills completely off, including our mortgage, and to have enough money to just breathe!" That must have been the correct answer! Because it was just moments later that the same voice instructed me to place the date that I wanted to completely pay off the bills on the envelopes right under the stamp. It's funny how desperation will cause people not to question their actions but become totally obedient. Right then and there, I did exactly as I was instructed. I placed a date three months away from that day under the stamp of every bill we had, including our mortgage! Then with an unexplainable peace, I finally went to bed.

The very next day, while outside talking to a neighbor, I noticed a "For Sale" sign on a home across the street. When my neighbor informed me of the sale price, my mouth dropped open and I knew exactly what we were about to do. I went in the house, called my husband at work, and told him that I thought we should sell the house. I explained to him what happened the night before while sitting at the glass table. I also told him the asking price for the house across the street. Of course, his response was, "We can talk about it when I get home." However, after some hesitation, a lot of discussion, and much prayer, we did it! We both knew that this was our divine intervention! We decided to put our home, which we loved so much but could no longer afford, up for sale. Once the decision was made, a feeling of peace replaced the anxiety. We had never sold a home before, but within days, we found the perfect realtor. The process played out on fast-forward from there. So fast that it made our heads spin! I love color and my sister once told me that my walls looked like a bag of Skittles had exploded on them! I had also watched way too much HGTV and painted the kitchen cabinets blue. I even spray painted my refrigerator and stove silver because I wanted stainless steel appliances and I couldn't afford them. Yes, I did that! And yes, the first time I cooked and cleaned my stovetop, all the paint came off, exactly like my husband said it would. In order to get top dollar for our home, it took about a month to prepare our house to be listed on the market. We had one open house and our property sold one day later! We went to settlement weeks later. We walked away from the sale with enough money to pay every bill we had! To our amazement, it was almost the exact date that I had written on all the envelopes! We also had money to spare. We paid for a full year's rent on an apartment,

29

bought a reliable car, put the rest in savings, and we *breathed again*! I thanked God for hearing and answering my prayer that night. ✓

While in my crisis, I had no idea that giving up a home that we worked so hard to get and to keep would bring so much financial peace, but it did. We had to be willing to lose in order to gain. Years later, during the Moneywise Empowerment seminars, I would hear Kelvin Boston say not to wait until the bank comes and takes your home away. He said to sell it and walk away before it was taken from you. He stated that you can get another house and informed the audience that wealthy and business-savvy people did it all the time without hesitation. However, before this experience, I always had the mindset that you held on until your furniture was on the sidewalk and the locks were put on your doors. Anything less meant that you had not tried hard enough. I had no idea that rich people ever had to let go of or walk away from anything. I would learn that rich people have filed for bankruptcy, made bad investments, taken great risks, and walked away to avoid drowning in debt. For them, the possibility of loss was written into the equation from the onset. However, the goal is always to gain more than you lose and to learn from your mistakes.

There would be other "round glass table" moments in my life, but none as devastating as this one. You see, I learned more with each financial traumatic event. This experience made me smarter, wiser, and able to make better choices. Our credit that had been "hemorrhaging" would turn around with diligence and hard work. Our credit score was over 750 a couple of years after selling our home. We would later go on to purchase other homes and cars but with the power of *knowing more*. But even with this newfound knowledge, I also learned that there will still be moments of financial ups and downs. We would purchase our second home in 2007 at the beginning of the epic housing crisis, which most Americans never saw coming. We would later find ourselves severely upside-down in our mortgage. My husband and I could have easily become financially retraumatized and fallen into despair but instead, we took what we had learned and applied it. We were proactive and met the problem head-on. When restructuring our mortgage loan was not an option (because up to that point we had never missed or been late with a mortgage payment), we looked for other options. There were no feelings of hopelessness for me this time. I was "poor know more" and I knew that there was a solution for our problem. I just had to find it. I did not feel alone because there were so many people in our same predicament and this time, we talked to others about it. I did not feel the shame and loneliness that I experienced while going through bankruptcy. Also, by this time, I was traveling with Moneywise and had access to a plethora of people well-versed in finance and the housing market. Our best option was a short sale, which was a very tedious process of many ups and downs, but it worked out in the end. Although our credit was hit once again, it was not as bad as a foreclosure would have been. As I was on the road giving inspiration to others going through financial hardship, I was experiencing hardships of my own. But I knew that it would work out for me and I wanted to convince others that it would work out for them also. I wanted to give hope by sharing my journey. I was often told by attendees that they felt connected to my words because of my story. They said that it gave them hope for their financial situation.

Wealthy people are proactive. They never give up! They take advantage of laws and programs, including everything from bankruptcy to foreclosure, to pull themselves back up again without apology. I have heard them say, "I have made a lot of money and I have lost a lot of money, but I'm not worried because I made it once and I will make it again." That is a wealthy mindset! People who don't "know more" allow the shame and fear of their current situation to stop them from bouncing back and trying again. They feel that a bankruptcy, loss of a home, or bad credit are struggles that they cannot overcome. But I am here to share with you that you can overcome it! Even if your current financial situation is a direct result of your recklessness in handling your finances, do not let that stop you from learning the lesson and trying again. Failure only exists when you stop trying. A wealthy mindset never gives up! As my great friend and mentor, motivational speaker Dr. Willie Jolley says, "A setback is a setup for a comeback!" And come back we did, over and over again! And so can you! Make your round glass table moment one of your most valuable life lessons. Use the despair and desperation to open yourself up to learning a new way. Be willing to let it all go and take risks. Use your faith to empower you to make a radical leap for change! Your financial peace depends on it.

Know more:

- *Sometimes the only way to hold on is to let go.*
- *A success by any other name is still a success.*
- *Set financial goals and put a date on them.*
- *A house you can't afford will feel like a prison, not a home.*
- *Hope is a wealthy mindset.*
- *Hopelessness fuels poverty.*

Lesson 4

THEY CAN SEE YOU COMING

"I was running away,
Seemed my life was growing lower every day.
So, I searched the world to find some relief and peace of mind."

My husband and I were a one-car family for many years after getting married. Grocery shopping was within walking distance for me and I think my daughter's stroller had almost as many miles on it as our car's tires. Then when my girls started school, they took the bus and we made being a one-car family work. We owned a total of two cars during the early years of our marriage. The first one was a car that my husband had driven since he was a teenager, and when we got married, his father gave it to us. I'll never ever forget that sky blue Plymouth Valiant with the door that would open unexpectedly when you made a left turn. It also had a broken gas gauge which caused my mother much concern.

So much so that she insisted on stopping to get gas while driving me to the hospital when I was in labor with our first child. That was the longest five minutes of my life! But that car took us from North Carolina to Texas and up and down the East Coast many times before dying a slow and tedious death. Our next automobile was a Chevrolet Monte Carlo that we purchased from my brother. It was quite an upgrade from what we were used to. It was beautiful with its soft leather seats and so much larger than our first car. It also gave us many years of service, but the maintenance that it required before it was no longer drivable was very costly. However, when this car died, the timing could not have been worse. My husband had recently changed jobs and his commute went from a 15-minute drive to almost two hours one way. We were in desperate need of a car and we were about to have our first interaction with buying a car through a dealership.

I had seen an ad on television that said this particular dealership could get anyone into a new car, no matter what their credit looked like. They also required no down payment. I'll never forget walking into the dealership with all its shiny new and used cars in the showroom and that new car smell! My husband and I were still quite young, in our twenties. I can't imagine the look we must have had on our faces as we walked through the door with two young children in tow. We desperately needed transportation and I am sure we had the look of desperation on our faces. We were greeted by a large, tall salesman. I will never forget how he seemed to tower over us, but he was professional and kind. After a brief conversation about why we had come into the dealership, he assured us that we could get into a car that night. The prospect of driving a new car home made us very hopeful and excited. He said that he understood our situation and had helped many people in similar situations get into a new car. Before looking at any cars, he had us fill out a credit application, which made me a little uncomfortable because I knew we had some late payments during the time that my husband was unemployed. So, it was no surprise when the salesman came to us and said that it would be difficult to get us into a new car but asked if there was a used car that we liked. We chose a blue Dodge Omni. We knew nothing about these cars except that this one was much smaller than the gas-guzzling Monte Carlo that we had. It was also one of the cheapest cars on the lot. We test-drove it and decided that it was the one we wanted to buy.

The salesman told us that we would need to make a sizable down payment, since our credit was not good, and we did not have much established credit. He then used the "I have to see if my manager will go along with this deal" statement. After what seemed like hours, he came back to tell us that the manager said

37

it's a "no-go". We were devastated because we had given them the "sizable down payment" he had asked for. However, it was what happened next that took my husband and I both by surprise. The salesman came back and said that he could "personally" get the deal to go through but it would take an additional $400 in cash. We did not understand why we needed to put down more money and especially why it had to be in cash. However, we went along with it because we desperately needed a car and he was promising to put us in a car by the next day. We never even thought about investigating other options because we thought we had none, considering our credit issues. We thought that we would run into the same issue no matter where we went. We had no knowledge or experience in purchasing a new vehicle. We also did not have enough money to purchase a car in cash and we were told that paying over time would help improve our credit score. So, the following evening, we were back at the dealership with $400 in cash. The salesman escorted us back into his office. We were seated at the table and asked if we had brought the cash. When my husband attempted to hand him the money, the salesman insisted that it be placed in his hands from under the table, literally. Despite being very naive about the car-buying process, it was at that point that I knew this transaction was not appropriate. The transaction made me feel dirty and taken advantage of, and it still arouses uneasy emotions as I write about it today. I now know that the salesman literally saw our need and desperation coming through the door. He had to have seen the word "suckers" written on our foreheads. We ended up with a car after putting down almost $1500, which was more than half, and still needed some dear friends to co-sign for the car loan. We were sold a lemon that night, and we had many mechanical issues for the entire time that we owned the car. Our desperation had lead the way and he saw us coming. But we dealt with it and made every single payment on time for the two years that we had the car. The only positive result that came out of the experience was that our credit score did increase from making the car payments on time and we also learned a very valuable lesson. We never wanted to be taken advantage of like that again.

I have learned that people can see you coming, whether you are poor, wealthy, or anything in between. While traveling with the wealthy men and women of the Moneywise Tour, I began to notice similarities in how they conducted and carried themselves. There was a confidence and an air about them. It was not flamboyance but a very subdued power. It may have been the pen that they wrote with or the simple watch that they wore on their wrist. Sometimes it was just a glance that they gave to one another. The wealthy just seemed to know wealth. Now I am not talking about the rich and famous that we see on television that scream, "Look at me! I have money!" Or the ones who have large entourages of people around them, jewelry hanging from everywhere, big expensive cars, and first-class everything. No, this wealth is quiet and very unassuming, yet other wealthy people can see them coming without a word. A perfect example of this occurred while I was singing in Palm Beach, Florida. My husband and I had the opportunity to dine at a very upscale restaurant in a very posh section of town. As we approached the hostess, I noticed that they had tables right next to these large open windows that offered wonderful views of the decorated shops. I stood there hoping that we would get one of those tables. Just at that time, an older couple entered the restaurant. They had this unexplainable air about them. They were modestly dressed but I felt that his shirt alone probably cost more than everything my husband and I had on. The jewelry was simple but elegant and they spoke in a soft tone. With just a glance at the hostess, they were escorted to the very area that I hoped to sit in. Now, they may have had reservations, or they could have been regulars at the establishment. I do not know. What I *do* know is that there was a sense of expectation that exuded from them as they were taken to their table. We were eventually called to be seated, and when I asked the hostess if we could sit next to the window, she said yes. As I sat at our table, excited that what I had hoped for came true, I began to think about the difference between a hope and an expectation. I stood at the hostess' desk wanting a particular table but not knowing if I could have it. Whereas the other couple entered the restaurant and approached the hostess' desk knowing that they would be given the best seat in the house. I knew that night that I wanted to learn how to live with expectation and not hope alone.

It would be a couple of years before we were ready to purchase another car. However, this time, I was also employed, and our credit score had risen sharply with much diligence and hard work. When we entered the car dealership, we had already been approved through our credit union. We had also educated ourselves on a great price for the car we wanted. I was armed with my spreadsheet of information on the cost of the upgrades that I wanted, too. I felt so empowered that I wanted my daughters, who were now in middle school, to see the right way to purchase a car. I did not want them to ever be targeted the way we had been. I wanted them to have a new homeschool lesson in finances and to know more. We purchased the car that we wanted that day. We did not sit there waiting for hours while the salesman played the "dealership game." We negotiated what we knew to be a fair price and we were ready to take our business elsewhere if we were not happy. We did not need a co-signer and we put zero down. I felt vindicated! However, I must admit that some of the residue from being taken advantage of was still on my mind. Actually, I never want all of the residue to completely go away. I want to remember that feeling of desperation. I now use that memory to push me to know more and do more to help myself and others. It also reminds me that I want to repeat the mistakes of my past "no more." Since that time, we have purchased our last four automobiles with zero down payment and a zero-percent finance charge. Yes, it can be done. Yes, it feels great to walk into a place expecting to be approved for what you want and need. Although we can, we don't go for the items at the top of our budget. We love the peace of living within our means. You should never want anything so bad that you ignore that little knot in your stomach that's telling you, "This is not a good financial decision." Be willing to walk away, even if you feel that you are in dire need. There is always an alternative, even if it means waiting and sacrificing some comfort, such as having to take public transportation.

You must learn to move beyond your desperation into hope, and then expectation. Educate yourself before making a move. Ask for insight from people who have gotten to where you want to be. Read and do your research. Make patience your friend. Try not to make quick, impulsive, or last-minute decisions when making a purchase. Be willing to sacrifice some comfort to get what is best for you. Also, make a promise to yourself that you will retain your dignity, even if you must leave without getting what you came for. Expect and demand to be treated professionally. If you currently find yourself in the middle of a bad deal that was made, make the most of it. Glean whatever you can from it while making the conscientious choice not to repeat the same mistake. Remember, our bad deal produced a better credit rating for us and a valuable lesson. Walk with a wealthy mindset, even if your bank account says otherwise! Even if you have not arrived yet, practice your walk, because they can see you coming.

Know this:

- _Walk like someone is watching you._

- _Hope is good, but expectation is great._

- _Make patience your friend._

- _Desperation opens the door for exploitation._

Lesson 5

HELLO, MY NAME IS BILL!

"The struggle ends with surrender, surrendering it all.
So, stop working against your destiny, stop running from your
call.
The struggle ends with surrender and I surrender all."

When I was a child, I had such a horrible interaction with a bill collector calling our home late one night for my parents that I vowed to never be traumatized like that again. How did I plan to do that? By ignoring the bill collector's calls. Okay, I had to learn this the hard way, and I pray that it helps someone today ... BILLS DON'T GO, THEY GROW! Ignoring bills will not make them go away. Instead, it makes them grow! How? Well, those interest charges, late fees, legal fees, and court costs continue to grow, and could result in garnishment of your paycheck and possibly rendering you unable to pay other bills and financial obligations. It robs you of your precious time, trying to dodge those debt collectors and hiding your automobile at friends' houses so it can't be repossessed. I don't even have to tell you how much it disrupts your peace! You dread answering your phone, getting your mail, or checking your email. It gets very embarrassing as the collectors begin contacting everyone that you used as a reference when they do not get a response from you. You make liars out of family and friends who say they have not heard from you. Most of all, having your power cut off or furniture put out on the street for lack of payment is a huge reality check. Then you become upset that your creditors are using every legal action at their disposal to get you to pay back money that you owe them. Only now, instead of owing them maybe $2,500, that debt has ballooned to $4,000. At this point, you are feeling totally frustrated and perhaps even angry or depressed. So, you seek relief by going shopping or out to eat because you don't have enough money to pay off that big bill anyway. The entire process begins to wear you down, making you feel hopeless and powerless. Sound familiar? Well, it certainly does to me because I have paid the fare to ride that bus more times than I care to remember. But I finally got wise and got off!

I found my "super power" when I decided to bite the bullet, get all my bills together, and make a plan to pay them off! I did it one bill at a time. It was one of the most difficult, tedious, yet rewarding things I have ever done. It took commitment and a daily sacrifice. I decided to stop letting creditors "spend my money" because they are already rich! I wanted to pay back what I owed and the interest that I agreed to pay for using their money, but that was it. I learned to use credit to *my* advantage instead of it being solely to *their* advantage. Taking control of YOUR money is one of the most MATURE and EMPOWERING feelings in the world!

I began my journey by not waiting for creditors to call me. Instead, I took a deep breath and called them! I took the bull by the horns and faced my greatest fear. I decided to make advocates of those I felt were adversaries. Having worked in collections in the past, I knew that I could either get a collector with no compassion or one filled with compassion like I was. I knew that the personalities could differ greatly but they all had the same goal: to resolve the debt. I called them every month to let them know when they could expect my payment. I also let them know if a payment might be late or short. I explained to them that it was my goal to pay off the debt as soon as possible and I solicited their assistance. I made sure that I addressed them by name and I tried to speak with the same person each time. Debt collectors can be your advocate because they have knowledge about the process that you may be unaware of. They can assist you with possibly writing off some or all of the penalties or interest, or even settling the account for less than the amount owed. This has the potential of saving quite a bit of money while attempting to pay off debt. I also knew that I had the option of requesting a different debt collector if I so desired. They are people, too, some with personal financial problems of their own. In the end, once I was resolved to reach my newly-established goals of getting out of debt, no debt collector was going to prevent that.

I organized my bills, started with the one that had the lowest balance and paid that one off first. Seeing a bill stamped "Paid in Full," even if it was just a $20 doctor's bill, gave my financial confidence a boost that let me know I could do this. I then took that extra $20 per month and added it to the payment for paying off the next bill with the lowest balance. Fighting the temptation to reward myself by spending the extra $20 per month on something I wanted was extremely difficult at times. However, this is where maturity, dedication, and determination to reach my goal had to kick in. Once I paid the smaller bills off, I began to tackle the bills with the highest interest rates. All the extra money from the paid bills went into paying off another outstanding bill. During this time, I still paid the minimum due on all the other bills. I paid every bill that I had, one bill at a time, in the same manner, until they were all paid off. I accomplished my goal in half the time using this method. I can't explain the overwhelming feelings of accomplishment, empowerment, and victory! I had chiseled through that mountain of debt one bill at a time until it existed no more. The entire process was tedious and took quite some time. I reminded myself that I did not get into this position overnight and although I wanted to, I would not get out of it quickly either.

However, going through the process was lifechanging because of the knowledge and understanding that I acquired and what I learned about myself. I discovered that I *did* have the stamina, perseverance, determination, and ability to change my financial behavioral patterns. The things that I felt I needed so badly that I was willing to go into debt for I either did not want any more or learned to wait for. My spending patterns changed, and I developed new, improved, and responsible lifelong spending habits. I truly learned the difference between want, need, and impulse buying. The word "credit" was no longer something to fear or avoid because I learned to make it work for me. Now, I keep my balances to an amount I can pay off in no more than three months. I have two or three credit cards and I turn down offers for all the rest unless it is a ridiculously low fixed interest rate.

Today, I remember being a homemaker with very limited funds. For many years, I used to think that having a wallet full of credit cards meant that I had arrived into a particular status in the world. After becoming employed outside my home, I applied for every store and bank credit card that I was offered. I remember one day spreading all my credit cards on my bed and rolling around on them like I was in some sort of Hollywood movie! I was filled with pride because they all had only my name on them. I thought that these plastic cards meant that I had "made it," although I did not know what "it" was. I was financially immature. What I had made was a Hollywood horror story and an enormous mistake that would take me years to correct. But I did it! I got out from under the bus that hit me! I went from feeling powerless and hopeless to feeling empowered! Now, I not only help myself, but I also help others. I became that advocate that I had once so desperately needed. What was such a dark place in my life is now being used as a beacon of light for others to know that it can be done. Ultimately, the greatest gift of all is the newfound peace that I have obtained through knowledge and wisdom. This wealth of peace is absolutely priceless!

<u>*Know More:*</u>

- *Bills don't go, they grow.*
- *Immaturity will get you into debt, but maturity will get you out of it.*
- *Learn the rules of the credit game and then become an expert at playing it.*
- *You can change your financial story from one of chaos to one of peace.*

Lesson 6

THE STRENGTH IN YOUR VALLEY

"You go on and be strong.

You'll find strength, just hold on.

Just look to the sky, you won't die.

Just keep on climbing!

You'll find strength in your valley!"

I did not know what to expect during my first Moneywise Empowerment Seminar. The first city that I participated in was Baltimore, Maryland, which was my hometown. I thought to myself, *"This is not going to be like singing in churches or at faith-based conferences."* I would be performing at a corporate event with sponsors from large financial institutions. I was not sure which songs would be appropriate to sing as I looked through my catalog of music tracks. I thought I would keep it light, very polished, and not too deep. So, I was quite surprised when Mr. Kelvin Boston requested a song that I had written entitled, "Strength in the Valley." The song was written during a very difficult time in my life. I had never sung this song in a setting such as the one I was currently in and I questioned Mr. Boston's song of choice. However, he was very clear on what he wanted me to sing.

I had written this song many years ago while working in a hospital as an Occupational Therapy Assistant. The financial challenges that my husband and I were facing at the time were taking their toll on our mental, emotional, and even physical well-being. I was caring for one of my patients, Miss Kathy, whom I had come to love dearly. She was an elderly woman who had raised three amazing daughters on her own while being almost bed-bound for many of those years. She was feisty, funny, and she had a voice like an angel! Miss Kathy would make me sing with her and to her on a daily basis. Initially, I felt awkward and shy singing for her, but she never took no for an answer. If I entered her room, I knew that I was not going to get back out the door before singing a song or two! I loved it most on the days that she would sing along with me. She challenged me in music in a way that I had never been challenged before. As her health began to fail even more and her level of participation decreased, she was removed from my caseload. However, I would follow her as she moved from one hospital unit to another. When she fell into a coma, I followed her into intensive care. She and I had formed a very close and loving relationship. I could not let a day go by that I did not go to her bedside to sing to her. After she slipped into a coma and I was not sure if she even knew I was there, I softly sang into her ear. I had become very attached to her, but I would not know just how much until later. While driving home from work one Friday, I felt in my heart that I had seen Miss Kathy for the last time. I wanted to turn my car around to be by her side. I began to cry and think about how she needed me during her time in the hospital. I had been there to give her therapy, hold her hand, sing with her, or just bring a little joy to her day. Suddenly, I clearly heard the words, "She did not need you. You needed her strength." As I thought it over, I realized that every day from her bed and in her valley experience, she was giving *me* strength. I was overcome with emotion and in the midst of my tears, I began writing the song, "Strength in the Valley." The words and the melody were coming even as I drove my car crying, filled with grief and gratitude. It is a song about finding your strength even in your darkest hour. It speaks about knowing that you have everything you need to succeed, even when you can see nothing there. It's a song about the power of God's peace, joy, and love, being in the midst of life's most difficult circumstances. It is also a song that combats the feelings of helplessness, hopelessness, and loneliness. It speaks to all the emotions that often accompany great losses in life, be they death, divorce, or finances.

On my first day of the tour, I was ready to be all business. I still did not understand Mr. Boston's choice of songs for a financial empowerment tour, but he was the boss. A video on depression and finance-induced stress was played. Following the video, a presenter addressed how financial problems can rob a person of their joy, strength, and hope, even leading some to suicide. I personally knew what it felt like to be in the grips of a financial horror story and to be overwhelmed with feelings of hopelessness and despair, with seemingly no way to escape. I had witnessed the tension and arguments between spouses in the offices of bankruptcy attorneys. These financial issues had driven many of them from bankruptcy court right into divorce court! I knew that for my husband and I, it was our faith in God that held our marriage and our minds together. However, even with my faith and my beliefs, there were times when I didn't know if I had the strength to make it through my own "valley experiences." So, it was with all those emotions, memories, and thoughts going on inside me that I then heard my name being introduced to the audience by Mr. Boston. As I approached the microphone, the room grew silent. During my first Moneywise Empowerment

Seminar, I sang from the part of my heart that contained all the emotions I felt when I first wrote the song. To my surprise, as well as to others in the audience, the tears began to flow down the faces of some of the attendees and presenters. Some let them flow freely, while others desperately fought back their tears. We were all taken by surprise. Attendees would later tell me that they did not know they would face those types of emotions in a financial seminar.

Financial stress brings much grief to those who are bound by it. With its bondage often comes a sense of hopelessness, sadness, anxiety, and fear. We have all heard the stories of those feelings of doom following a traumatic financial event. The stressors may include but are not limited to: the loss of a job, a business, or a home, large amounts of money, or other financial traumas. I refer to it as FTS, or "Financial Traumatic Stress." Although I did not initially understand Mr. Boston's motives, it soon all made sense to me. He understands that being wealthy is a holistic approach and the emotional ties to finances must be addressed in order to have hope for a change. Hopelessness is a dream-killer. My songs seemed to touch the very heart of the matter for many people in attendance. Hearts were opened up to receive and minds were opened up to believe that there was hope for their financial situations. It was then that I realized my purpose in the seminar was much more than to simply entertain with a song or two. I was there to inspire people to hope, expect, and dream again! That day, I had a flashback to the time I was sitting in my car crying before my bankruptcy hearing and asking God, "Why am I going through this?" At that very moment, it all made sense again as I heard the words, "This is your ministry." If I were to choose one comment that is heard over and over again at the Moneywise Empowerment Seminars, it would be, "I did not expect to feel this way at a conference on finances!"

Everything in your life can ultimately be used to benefit you, if you know what to do. Financial stumbling blocks can either be used to trip you up and make you fall, or help you step up to a higher place. Finances do not define a person's value in life. If allowed, the lack of hope will rob us of the precious gift of time that could be spent being productive and impacting the lives of others. The power of knowing beyond what you are seeing and facing can build your life into a legacy. Miss Kathy's life, although she battled illness for many years and functioned in what appeared to be a hopeless valley experience, has instead become a legacy of strength, endurance, hope, and love for me and many others. Being moneywise will teach you to gather your strength, dust off your dreams, and position yourself to increase in knowledge and wealth. You can say that you will be "poor no more" because you will know more! You can find your strength in your valley.

Know more:

- *Hopelessness is a dream-killer.*
- *The only way to lose and win at the same time is to give.*
- *The only limitation placed on God is your faith.*
- *Everything you need to change your financial situation is available to you.*
- *You are much stronger than your weaknesses.*

Lesson 7

GOING SCARED

"I stepped out of my boat filled with doubt beyond reason.
And I walked on the water into my brand-new season.
I kept my eyes on Him and I did not sink.
And now I'm blessed more than I can think."

I sang my first solo onstage in front of more than a thousand people when I was just nine years old. The church was packed! I recall all eyes being on me as I walked to the front of the church and up the steps, where I was handed a microphone. I had told my mother weeks before that I wanted to sing at this service in our new church. I had lead the choir in songs before at the small church that we previously attended. However, this time there would be no choir standing behind me, so all the attention would be on me. I had practiced the cutest song that my cousin thought would be perfect for a little girl like me. However, I had no intention of singing that song. It was way too "babyish" for my style! I had other plans for what I would sing. It was not until I turned and faced the audience that fear gripped me. I was not sure if I was going to be able to sing any song at all. The massive crowd stared at me and waited in anticipation for me to begin. There was no music. I would be doing this song a cappella, so it was all on me to start. I was gripped by fear and could not move. I could see my mother and cousin looking at me from the audience and it didn't help my fear at all. It was then that I closed my eyes and courage stepped in to overcome my fear. I could no longer see what was terrifying me, although I was aware that the people were still there. I opened my mouth and begin to sing the song that I had chosen for myself. By the time I reached the end of the song, there were musicians playing for me, a choir singing with me, and the entire church was up on their feet clapping for me! Decades later, as a professional singer, I still close my eyes before singing to find my courage and center myself. I never allow fear to stop me from doing what I need to do. I have performed while scared many times. I just take my fear along with me and wait for the entrance of courage to conquer the fear.

There have been times when I have operated in fear with respect to my finances. Suffering losses because of uneducated, impulsive, or just bad decisions have made me afraid to take part in anything I thought was financially risky behavior. I just wanted to take any money I did have and hide it under a mattress. However, through traveling with Moneywise, I would learn that investing in just about anything is a risky business. There is no sure thing in purchasing a home, starting a business, investing in the stock market or retirement funds, and even putting money in a bank. If a person is trying to make their money grow, they are taking a financial risk. Mr. Kenneth Brown, one of the youngest African American males to become wealthy through ownership of McDonald's restaurant franchises, has a saying, "Scared money can't make money!" He believes that if you hide your money under the mattress, you may not lose it, but you will not make it multiply either. Scared money also eventually turns into "spent money."

Fear concerning finances is very real and understandable, especially when you have lost a great deal, or even everything you had. However, the mindset of an enlightened and informed wealthy person is different from those who do not know more. During one of the Moneywise seminars, Mr. Kelvin Boston spoke of losing almost $600,000 in one year. He said that although it was very upsetting, he did not operate in fear because he believed that if he made it once, he could make it again. That type of loss would have haunted me for a lifetime and made me very afraid to invest in anything ever again. But when you know more, you understand that there are always gains and losses in finances. The ideal is that you will always gain more than you lose. However, the reality is that you may also lose greatly at times. Fear has always been an emotion that is meant to be conquered and overcome. Courage does not cancel out fear, but it enables one to keep going despite their fear. The only way to conquer fear in finances is to become educated and know how to make the most informed decisions and minimize the potential for loss. Mr. Boston was able to recoup his losses in a matter of months because he knew what to do and did it. He did not let fear and failure keep him from trying again.

Wealthy people study how to become and remain wealthy. They are voracious readers of anything that pertains to their business. They are also very inquisitive, asking questions of anyone and everyone whom they think may have information they can use. They surround themselves with like-minded people who have achieved goals they are trying to reach. Most importantly, they factor into the equation the possibility of losses from the beginning and use the experience as a lesson in what not to do next time. My amazing friend and mentor, Dr. Willie Jolley, who happens to be one of the most sought-after inspirational and motivational speakers in the world, coined a phrase: "A setback is a setup for a comeback!" This is an awesome comeback for dealing with fear! It teaches us that we can use our fear and our failures to set us up to be better positioned financially in the future. For the people who lack this knowledge, fear will incapacitate them in their finances. But for those who know more, fear may inspire them. During a stock market crisis, when the majority of investors are pulling their money out of stocks, savvy and fearless investors are pouring their money in. Their fearless investing has made millionaires into multimillionaires and billionaires. Whatever your financial goals are, educate yourself on what you are trying to achieve. Create a plan that includes the potential for gains and some losses. Decide if you will be led by fear or courage. And if all else fails, close your eyes and sing your way though it!

Know this:

- *Courage helps you face your fear.*
- *Use fear and failures to set you up, not set you back.*
- *Any business is risky business.*
- *Sometimes, you must go scared.*
- *Failure is a new starting point.*

Lesson 8

YOU NEVER KNOW WHO'S IN THE ROOM

"There's standing room no matter how late you come.
There's standing room though we've already begun.
You may not be able to sit down at the table,
but you must come through the door."

The call came in at 11:30 pm on a Friday night. A stranger on the other end had been given my contact information by a mutual acquaintance. He wanted to know if I could sing at his client's funeral on Wednesday. I was not used to getting calls for booking inquiries at 11:30 at night on my private line but I listened to what he had to say because of my relationship with the person who had recommended me. The call was almost like an interview, as he told me what would be required of me. He also had questions about my fees and song selection. The last question he asked was whether I would agree to sing, and I did agree to it the following day. A week later, I was at the church early in the morning, ready to sing at the funeral of someone I did not know and had never heard of before. I arrived an hour early and took the liberty of reading the obituary. I discovered that the deceased was in his 70s, a beloved husband, father, and grandfather, and a businessman. The sanctuary of the church was somber and filled with people there to pay their final respects.

As I gazed around the church, I looked for faces I recognized and found two people I knew. I saw a few more faces that looked familiar, although I could not recall where we had met. After I sang my first song, a small group of people began to speak about their relationship with the deceased. As I read the list of names on the program, I recognized a couple of them as being very wealthy and influential people in the African-American community, such as Mr. Bob Johnson, Ms. Cathy Hughes, and Ms. Debra Lee. I then realized that a few of the faces in the church looked familiar to me because I had seen them on television. By now, I was starting to feel a little intimidated as they called me up to sing my next and final song. I knew that there was a great deal of wealth in the room, with at least two people that I knew for sure were billionaires! However, I managed to keep my focus on the family and the task at hand. I was contracted to sing one last song, "Great Is Thy Faithfulness".

However, after hearing how many people the deceased had helped when no one else would invest in their dream, I knew that he had been the wind beneath so many wings in that room! So, I followed my heart instead of doing as instructed and went right into the song "Wind Beneath My Wings," but kept it very short. Hearts were filled as the tears flowed throughout the church during that song. I have learned that following my heart may be risky, but it is often a risk worth taking. I would later find out that the only disappointment that the family had in me was that I did not complete the entire song. The song was such a great representation of the life of their loved one and what he meant to so many people in that church. The lobby of the church after the services looked like a "Who's Who?" among the rich and powerful. They were multimillionaire and billionaire entrepreneurs in the telecommunications field. What they all shared was they had all been given their start-up monies by the man to whom they had just paid their final respects. They had gathered on the same day in the same place, and because I answered a call at 11:30 at night, I also sat among them. My gift had made room for me to sit and to sing in the presence of some very great and powerful people.

I would later get a call from the woman who had referred me, who is a very powerful woman in her own right, to say how deeply the family and others in attendance had been touched by my music. However, it was her next question that would leave me speechless! She asked, "Doreen, what do you need to take your music to the next level?" She stated that she had contacts and partnerships with people who were in the church that day whom she felt might be willing to assist me in getting what I needed to reach my potential. She called it the "Billionaire Corner." I had never been asked, point-blank, by anyone what I needed to reach my goals. No one with connections and contacts to wealth had ever told me to pray so we would both know how God wanted to use them to help me. I honestly was not ready for the opportunity that was being presented to me and did not have an immediate answer to her question. Up until that time, my thinking process had been limited to what I knew I could afford to accomplish through my own finances, efforts, and limited connections. I was raised to think that if you use your own money and your own time, you will owe no one. I always thought that if I could not afford it, then it was not meant for me to have. Asking for help was not an option that I was taught or even wanted to take. At that time, I had not yet learned the lesson or the necessity of partnerships. I had not fully comprehended that some of the richest people in the room that day had started out with nothing but a dream. They thought enough of their dream and their future value to ask for and accept help. They partnered what they had to offer in their future with someone else who had more to offer today. My thinking was "stinking" in that I thought I had to do it all myself and to accept help was a weakness and too much of a risk. So, I operated from a standpoint of what I could do with the money that I had, which would not take me far at all. I needed help and she saw that. I also needed confidence and solid goals and she soon saw that, too. I could not answer her question of what I needed to go to the next level. I realized that although I had immense talent and a wonderful opportunity being presented to me, I was not prepared for it. I had spent my time in music preparing for the small and not the extraordinary. I had short-term goals but no long-term vision. I had no written mission statement or vision statement to follow. I did a lot of hoping but my expectations were limited. I had no idea of my true value as an enterprise and not just a singer. I lost out on an opportunity of a lifetime because I was not prepared. It is one thing to have your gift and talents exposed to great people and quite another to know what to do with the exposure to create your dream. But now I "know more" and I plan to lose "no more" opportunities in the future. This chapter is for those of us who do not have our 30-second elevator speech together. This is your personal commercial in 30 seconds or less. It's for those of us who think that we must get it done alone and not ask or expect help. That way, if we fail, we have failed on our own time and with our own money. It's also for those of us who severely underestimate our value and what we bring to the table. Most of all, it's for those of us who don't fully believe there is someone who is willing to back our dreams. Everyone has a starting point. The dividing factor is what one group knows and believes that the other group *doesn't* know and believe. Take a chapter out of my book and be prepared for when you are "in the room" and ready to answer the *question*. Room has already been made for you in this world. It is just waiting for you to come fill your place. Like the missing piece of a puzzle, you will fill it perfectly. Your value is there. Your gift has carved out a space for you. But you must be ready!

Know more:

- _You were not created to be small!_
- _Lack of preparation leads to deprivation._
- _Prove that you are ready._
- _Accepting help is not a weakness._
- _Be prepared always._

Lesson 9

THE PRINCIPLE OF PARTNERSHIP

"You're the one.

The one to share my dreams.

The one I've been looking for.

The one who understands me.

I thank God for breathing you on me."

There is a wonderful story in the Bible. In the book of Exodus 17:12, it reads: *"However, Moses' hands grew heavy; so, they took a stone and put it under him, and he sat on it. Aaron and Hur held up his hands, the one on the one side and the other on the other, so that his hands stayed steady until sunset."* The children of Israel were in a fierce battle with their enemies and as long as Moses' hands were raised, they were winning, but when Moses dropped his hands, they would begin to lose the fight. Moses was old and getting very tired of standing and he was losing the strength to keep his hands raised in the air. Aaron and Hur, who were much younger, were on the mountain next to Moses. They saw what was happening and jumped into action. They knew that if things continued as they were going, their army would lose the war. So, they quickly found a rock to sit Moses on and then took on the responsibility of keeping Moses' hands raised in the air until sunset. This act helped their soldiers win a very important victory for their people! Moses, although now old in body, was still rich in wisdom and he had the power of God in him to enable the soldiers to fight harder. Aaron and Hur had youth, strength, and the knowledge to think on their feet to keep Moses in position. This is a perfect example of a partnership. Three individuals working together towards the same goal resulted in victory for thousands of people.

Pairing our gifts, talents, knowledge, wealth, wisdom, time, and finances together creates a much stronger chord than the individual who is trying to do it all alone. Enlightened people know the value of helping one another for the greater good. This knowledge, along with being connected to like-minded people, has led many to great wealth and power. They understand the concept that "no man is an island. No man stands alone." And in a true partnership, everyone benefits from teamwork. It takes humility to form great partnerships. Everyone must know and respect one another's strengths and weaknesses for them to work. Moses had to admit that he was old and did not have the physical strength and power that he once had. Aaron and Hur had to accept the fact that although they were physically strong, they lacked the spiritual power and wisdom that Moses still possessed. The opposite of this theory is to divide and conquer. There is a greater chance of failure and defeat when division finds its way into an effective partnership. Suppose Aaron and Hur could not agree on helping Moses. It would have been catastrophic! But instead, they both acted quickly by working together. As a result, many lives were saved that day. There is an African proverb that states, "If you want to run fast, run alone. If you want to run far, run together." After years of trying to do everything in music and business on my own, I realized that I could only get so far. There is great power and wealth to be achieved by those who know the value of a strong working partnership.

I had what I would consider a good amount of success early on after the release of my first CD. I met some major gospel artists. I was being invited to sing in various churches and conferences throughout the country, I was getting some radio airplay, and I was nominated for a Stellar Award. For someone who began with just a dream of having her own CD, this was quite an accomplishment and a very exciting time for me. Since I did not have the backing of a record label, every accomplishment was a major feat, and I was proud of the fact that, aside from family, I was basically doing this on my own. I was independent and making it happen. However, I would reach a point when, although what I deemed as success was still coming, it was coming at a much slower pace than I desired. My husband was my manager, webmaster, graphic designer, and booking agent. We were also both still working full-time jobs. Committing to concentrating on just growing the music business often took a backseat to the energy and money needed to pay the bills and keep our home running. Even if we wanted to, we could not afford to pay anyone for all the jobs that we were doing for our business. We also wondered who else we could trust with our dream. No one could possibly believe in us like we believed in ourselves. But we were completely wrong. There are times when others have believed in me **more** than I believed in myself! I would not see the power and necessity of partnerships until I started working with the Moneywise Empowerment Tour. I could have done so much more and gone so much farther, had I partnered with such a great team much earlier in my career. Also, since I did not understand what a partnership really was, I was too focused on what I would have to give up, as well as what I felt I lacked coming to the table. In general, I was not taught what it meant to strengthen myself through partnering with others.

The television show "Shark Tank" has become one of my favorite shows to watch. I used to wonder why the "Sharks" wanted such a large percentage of a company that they did not start and why the inventors were so willing to give it up. However, the more I watched, the more I understood that for many of the inventors, it was not just the money, it was the partnership. The inventors were willing to share the bottom line, which is the money, if the Sharks were willing to share their expertise and connections. They realized that they could earn a whole lot more money with one of the Sharks as their partner than they could ever make on their own. If a Shark wanted 30% of their company, that was the value that they were accessing for their time, talent, connections, and work. For the inventor, giving up some of their profits was just a part of the business deal. Partnerships are a give-and-take relationship. Now as with anything, there is the good and there is the bad. So, choose very wisely when entering a partnership. This decision should not be made because you are relatives or best friends, or even because of the availability of money. Like a marriage, it should not be entered lightly or emotionally. All partners must be accountable for doing their part, even when no one is looking. It is a mature relationship that should be entered with mature individuals who can carry their weight and do their part. There must be honesty, integrity, respect, and trust always! If not, the union is doomed from the start. Like a marriage, there's no greater heartbreak than seeing something fail that began with such hope, dreams, and expectations. A failed partnership can illicit some of the same emotions as a divorce and make one very leery about entering another one. Some disasters are unavoidable, but they can be used as great stepping stones to build the right partnership in the future. So, don't give up!

Through my travels with Moneywise, I have learned that money is not the greatest investment one may possess or give. Although money is undeniably a very important asset, there is still something greater in the community of these enlightened wealthy men and women, and that is time. Their time is a precious commodity that is allotted with just as much caution as their money. I have witnessed the power of partnership every time Mr. Kelvin Boston would announce another speaker or presenter that would be joining us on the tour in a particular city. It does not matter if it is one of the regular speakers, such as the amazing Dr. Willie Jolley, Dr. Dennis Kimbro, Robert Ferguson, Deborah Owens, or Kenneth Brown, or a guest speaker like John Hope Bryant, Peggy Duncan, or Gloria Mayfield Banks; their time is extremely valuable! Their time and knowledge are more valuable than any dollar amount that the Moneywise Tour could offer to them. Being able to call on some of the most gifted, talented, powerful, and respected people in their respective fields is an example of the fruits of the partnerships that Mr. Boston has developed with them. Having a front-row seat to this example has lead me to reevaluate my own partnerships. I am now looking at not only what others bring to the table of value but what am I bringing to the table as well. Partnership is a give-and-take equation. I must have something to give and my partner must have something I can use. If I am doing all the giving or doing all the taking, then it is not a partnership but rather a "dependency." Partnerships are always being reevaluated and reassessed to make sure that they are still working so that everyone is benefitting from the relationship. As in the story of Moses, if one of the partners need a little extra help, the others are right there to assist with whatever means necessary to reach the established goal.

Just as wealthy people know the value of a partnership that is working well on behalf of all involved, they also know when it is no longer working. They understand the value of "no" and although they may remain cordial and even friends, they do not hesitate to dissolve the partnership when it has been proven that it is no longer profitable for all parties involved. However, should another opportunity come along later to work as a team again, it will be revisited. The smart ones try not to burn any bridges and keep an open door of communication. I can now see how different the thought processes are between the wealthy, informed professional and the uninformed entrepreneur. When a person has little knowledge about business relationships, they tend to involve their feelings in the equation. The partnerships are often one-sided, with one person doing most of the giving and the other doing most of the taking. If one partner has all the money while the other has all the know-how and contacts, there may be an issue with the distribution of power when it comes to who has the final say in many decisions, especially those decisions relating to finances. We will not even discuss how complicated it may get when the partners are family members. It quickly becomes an affair of the heart. A "no" may turn into not speaking to one another, arguments, not showing up at the family reunion, kids not being able to play together anymore, divorce, or no more Sunday dinners together. It can get mighty rough, just like a divorce.

Here is a perfect example of a failed family partnership. There was a new soul food restaurant that opened in Baltimore that had some of the best food I had ever tasted this side of North Carolina! The menu consisted of items not seen in the other soul food eateries I had patronized in the area. It was so good that I told everyone I knew about it. I was their number one promoter. I would eat there at least twice a week and if I had family or friends come to visit, I took them there to eat also. I even convinced our entire office of therapists to have our luncheon there. Everyone was quite impressed. However, after a few months, I noticed that some of the counter workers that I was used to seeing were not there anymore. The ones that I knew who were still there were not as cordial as they used to be. The usual cashiers had been replaced with teenagers who obviously did not want to be there and would not know good customer service if it called them on the cell phone they were rudely speaking into while taking an order. The once-expansive menu seemed to be shrinking each time I visited. Then one day, I returned a food order because it was so badly prepared. My co-workers, some of whom had been eating there faithfully ever since our luncheon, had also begun to complain about the service and the food. It seemed like it wasn't a month later when this great soul food restaurant was closed. They were only in business for a little over three months from first opening their doors to closing them. What a shame, because on that side of town, there was no one who could come close to how great the food was. Before the restaurant closed, I had gotten the number of one of the cooks who worked there. He would later cater an event for my family. It was then that I found out what happened to cause this great family-owned business to close its doors in such a short amount of time. He explained to me that there was a personal disagreement between the co-owners, who were the cook and the business manager. That disagreement lead to a breakdown in the family and business partnership. This resulted in half the family leaving and taking all the cooks with them. The remaining partners attempted to prepare the food but were not cooks, so they scaled back the menu. The food was so bad that it was being returned by their patrons and the restaurant had developed a reputation of bad service and bad food. Ultimately, the restaurant closed. Family, friends, and business partners went their separate ways, having no further contact with one another. Unfortunately, this is not a rare occurrence, especially in small businesses. Just as you cannot have a defective product but great financial backing and succeed, you cannot have an excellent product with no financial backing and succeed either. The best formula to have in business is an excellent product supported by great financial backing. It takes maturity and a real commitment to work together through the highly profitable times, as well as the bumps in the road that are unavoidable. If you don't know more about business partnerships, and how and why they work, then when you get a "no" as an answer, it may destroy a partnership, a business, a friendship, and even a family. I have personally lived this experience, having been a child of family-run businesses. I have witnessed how ugly and messy a partnership can be when it's not working correctly. That is why I have tried so diligently to do it all on my own.

Now, thanks to my time with the Moneywise Empowerment Tour, as well as other life lessons, I have also witnessed what strong partnerships look like. When all hands are on deck doing their part, the partnership and the business is stronger. Braiding three ropes together to hold something is much stronger than using just one rope. You may be able to get the job done with just your single rope, but you will have to bear all the weight alone. You will sometimes be stretched so tight that you may feel like you are going to unravel. However, with the right partners, you are now stronger and able to accomplish so much more because the weight of responsibility is distributed amongst more people. There must be respect for what each individual brings to the table in a partnership. One of the greatest lessons that I have learned in my travels with Moneywise is the level of respect that everyone is given for what they bring to the tour. Although I may not be an expert in finances like Mr. Boston, or a great motivational speaker like Dr. Jolley, or a great educator and speaker like Dr. Kimbro, or a fitness guru like Mr. Ferguson, what I contribute is highly respected and celebrated by the team. You should never feel like the other partners are doing you a favor by "letting" you be a part of their group. You must know that what you are bringing to the team is valuable and needed to make the entire partnership work. It took me a while to grasp this concept because I felt like I was such a little fish being allowed to swim in a big ocean with all the great fish. I was not aware of my worth. It would be the respect and kindness given to me by the Moneywise team that let me know I was considered a true partner and, most importantly, that I belonged. This respect drives me to be better and to be an even stronger team player and partner. I want to always bring my portion of the rope to the table and stand ready to hold up someone's hand if necessary. Learning these principles of partnership has been one of the most valuable lessons for me.

Know more:

- _"If you want to run fast, run alone. If you want to run far, run together." – African Proverb_
- _Unity builds; division destroys._
- _Money and wisdom make a great partnership; it's being moneywise._
- _Choose your partners wisely._

Lesson 10

OWN SOMETHING

"There's a yielding in surrender
and the rendering of such peace.
The struggle ends, and the peace begins
when you yield at the Master's feet."

Everywhere we go for the Moneywise Empowerment Seminar, Mr. Kelvin Boston teaches that everyone should "own something." For many, that may begin with owning your own home. If you are paying to live in a condo, apartment, or house, you are either paying your own mortgage or someone else's mortgage. Homeownership is a privilege, a right, and a choice. My husband and I have owned three homes in our lifetime. One almost ended in disaster, one *did* end in disaster, and our present home is a redemption for the other two. However, we got smarter with each purchase. We were financed for our third home through a company called NACA (www.naca.com). We were able to secure our home with no down payment, no closing costs, no PMI, no second mortgage, and a fixed interest rate of 2.75%. Not even a low credit score can disqualify you from being approved for a home through NACA. Sounds too good to be true, doesn't it? Well, that is what holds many people back because they are waiting to hear the catch. However, there was no catch. You must complete their process and it is a *process* that tries hard to ensure that you are getting the home you can afford. But we did it and so can you. Some people would have never attempted homeownership again, following the rough ride that we had financially. However, my husband and I believe in home ownership and even with all its liabilities, purchasing our home is worth it to us.

The group of wealthy and wise individuals with whom I am very honored to travel as part of the Moneywise Tour stress repeatedly the importance of having "ownership" of something! Of course, owning your own home is a big one, but owning a business is stressed even more! In this economy, it is essential to have more than one stream of income. For most of us, gone are the days of retirement after working 30 years at a job and earning your gold watch and great pension. We now live in an "at-will" society where you may be released from your place of employment at any time for any reason, and unemployment is not a full paycheck. It should be noted that you do not have to quit your day job to have a second stream of income.

While traveling with the Moneywise tour, there were representatives from a large insurance company speaking about life insurance. They were part of a panel discussion on investing in life insurance as a stream of income. They stated that some people invest as a group, insuring the oldest member of their family with a large and expensive policy. When that family member dies, they are given a proper funeral and burial. They then invest the balance of the money into the family businesses and an insurance policy for the next-eldest family member. Money from a life insurance policy is not taxed. Some may see this as a little morbid. However, others see it as leaving a legacy.

How do you begin to find out what type of entrepreneur you should be? The possibilities are as endless as the unique gifts that God has given each and every one of us. Does everyone rave about how great your cooking or baking skills are? Does the artwork that you create when you do hair constantly bring compliments your way? Do you help friends through all types of situations with your wisdom? Or perhaps you have been told that you have an amazing business sense and can sell water to a fish in the ocean! Are you able to take everything in the house apart and put it back together again? Do you sing like a bird or tell jokes that have everyone holding the sides of their stomachs? Is there beautiful artwork on your walls that you have created? Or perhaps there is an inventor in you. I have learned that business-savvy people see income opportunity in just about everything. But how do you turn what appears to come so naturally for you into another stream of income?

I have found that the businesses we start for ourselves are not far from our heart or what we are naturally talented at doing. Dr. Dennis Kimbro states, "God gives us at least five-to-ten wealth-creating ideas in our lifetime but most of us disregard them and never act on them." Some of the people who follow through with these ideas are the ones you read about in money magazines. However, most successful business owners are leading very fulfilled lives outside of the public eye. For many of us, the only thing that stood between where Oprah Winfrey is and where we are is courage, faith, and action! We are all crafted to leave our unique impression and legacy on this earth. However, some people wake up and spend their days working to fulfill *their* ownership goals and others wake up and work to fulfill the goals of others. Entrepreneurship is a conscious decision that one makes to turn their gifts and talents into a business. You must first clear your mind of all the negative thoughts of what you were told you cannot do. Next, think of those things you know you are good at; the ones that come easy for you to do with excellence. It does not matter how big or small your business aspirations are. This is your dream. Take the limits off your mind and take a moment to dream beyond your current situation. Then start doing something right now … right where you are!

The Small Business Administration (SBA) has a wealth of information for setting up and even securing loans or grants for your business. You can find out more information and even find a counselor who will help you get started on their local website. There is special funding available for minorities and women through the SBA. Money is available for some of you in the form of loans or grants (which you do not pay back). Just be ready to roll up your sleeves and work the system. Anything in life worth achieving takes work, persistence, and commitment. You do not have to tackle this venture strictly from the standpoint of solely getting rich. If it turns into a wealthy place monetarily for you, then great! If it improves the quality of your life through an abundance of joy and fulfillment and gives you another stream of income, that's just as great! Everything does not have to be a full-fledged business to bring another stream of income and joy to your life. It's up to you how big or small you want to dream in your ownership of a home or business. To quote the Bible, *"To whom much is given, much is required."* That holds true for ownership. If you own much, then much upkeep will be required of you. The decision of how much you want and how hard you desire to work is all yours. This is the beautiful freedom of choice this life allows us.

Know more:

- _You are using your life to either build your own legacy or someone else's legacy._
- _Acting on your dreams makes them a reality._
- _Own something so you can leave something._
- _Put every gift you have to work._

Lesson 11

READING IS FUNDAMENTAL

"You are my why.

You are my when.

You are my how, both now and then.

All the questions I have in my life, the answer is You."

Poverty and wealth are learned behaviors. In life, you are either majoring in being poor, being rich, or somewhere in the middle. How and what you consume feeds into what your status is in life. There is one group of people who never read anything more than the words on their television screen. There is another group of people who buy and read the magazines found at the cash registers in supermarkets that have sensational headlines about the rich and famous. There is still another group of people whose reading material can be found in airports, libraries, and bookstores in the form of newspapers, books, and magazines.

93

Others only read stories found on the Internet. Lastly, there are those who rarely read anything at all. All these various groups read to gain some type of information. The question then becomes, where are you getting your financial information? How are you learning to be poor no more? You are reading material that will cause you to either spend money or material that instructs you on how to make and/or save money. Your reading material may be on how the stock market and real estate work or about what celebrity has the biggest house and the most money. You may read to invest and save, or you read to spend and consume. Perhaps you are getting your financial information through television programs or the Internet. Whatever your chosen format may be, the topics you know most about are the ones that you have read and studied the most.

Enlightened people of wealth read with the same passion and purpose that this generation applies when using their cell phones, participating in social media, or playing video games. To satisfy their reading compulsion, they are known to devour books, magazines, and periodicals back-to-back. The most interesting observation I have noticed is that none of their preferred reading materials are found at supermarket checkout counters and they are not easily accessed by the masses. Their preferred reading list includes books and articles about money, investments, empowerment, travel, and works that inspire and motivate.

Why is it that the magazines and reading materials that are most accessible to the under-served communities are not informative on finances or how to build wealth? What appears more accessible is literature that will get more money *out* of your pocket, not into it. Wealthy people make sound investments in themselves by taking the time to read material that will enlighten and empower them financially. They read to enrich their lives. They read material that will add knowledge and wisdom to their financial, professional, and life decisions. Reading is a passion of theirs and I personally see the impact that it makes on their lives. Most of them spend many more hours looking at printed material on paper or a computer screen than looking at images on a television. Many of them watch very limited hours of television. When traveling with the Moneywise group, their heads are often in a book or newspaper on planes, trains, and in automobiles. They never seem to arrive at the place where they know it all. There is always more to learn within the fluid world of finances. The take obtaining more knowledge very seriously.

Yes, to get where you want to go in life, reading the correct material is fundamental! Study what the successful people that you admire read and create your own lifechanging reading list. Start reading one article, one chapter, one newspaper at a time and start reading today! Pursue falling in love with reading to become more enlightened and acquire more knowledge and wisdom. Reading to expand their knowledge on a subject matter is a daily habit of the wealthy and wise. The ability to read is one of the greatest abilities in life. There is a reason why the right to learn how to read was forbidden for slaves. It is much easier to keep people in bondage when they cannot read. We often take reading lightly and for granted. However, what you are reading or not reading may be the difference between being wealthy or poor, or the difference between having peace of mind or living in chaos. Reading is fundamental to your financial growth. Don't let your lack of reading the right material keep you in financial bondage. Expand the library of your mind.

Know more:

- _Knowledge can build your life into a legacy._
- _People will teach you what they know and what they don't know._
- _Make frequent deposits into the library of your mind._

Suggested Reading:

- Who Moved My Cheese? _by Spencer Johnson, M.D._
- Rich Dad Poor Dad _by Robert T. Kiyosaki_
- The Millionaire Next Door _by Thomas J. Stanley and William D. Danko_
- Think and Grow Rich _by Napoleon Hill_
- The Wealth Choice: Success Secrets of Black Millionaires _by Dennis Kimbro_
- A Setback is a Set Up for a Comeback _by Willie Jolley_
- Who's Afraid to Be A Millionaire? _by Kelvin Boston_

Lesson 12

NOT THE SMARTEST COOKIE IN THE JAR

"There is greatness inside of me.
There is nothing that I can't be.
There is greatness inside of me."

During one of my early trips with the Moneywise Empowerment Tour, I found myself in a restaurant in Atlanta, GA with ten affluent and handsome African-American businessmen. All of them were very well-dressed in dark business suits and ties. Heads turned when they opened the door and entered the building. They all looked and smelled like success. They carried a very confident yet humble demeanor. They were all very well-spoken and conducted themselves as gentlemen, opening doors and pulling out chairs so I could be seated. Although I felt out of place, being the only woman in the group, I tried my best to appear like I belonged there, and I did.

Once seated, the conversation immediately took off. They began with a recap of the seminar that day; what went well and what could be improved. Whenever someone complimented or mentioned anything about my singing, I was brought into the conversation. They all felt that I added another dimension to the conference. However, that was the extent of my comfort level for participating in the conversation. It was not long before the discussion branched out into another direction that was way over my head. The men began to talk about franchises, hotel acquisitions, business dealings, and investments. I had absolutely nothing to add, and I felt incredibly dumb and out-of-place sitting among them. I quickly realized that the conversations I was privileged to hear were lifechanging and it was important for me to be quiet and listen. I sat there at this table of men, who were filled with financial wisdom, and tried to absorb as much as I could. Although it carries a negative connotation, not being the smartest cookie in the jar or not being the sharpest crayon in the box can be a very positive thing, as it turned out to be for me that night.

As I read my menu, trying to decide what I wanted to order, these men read through the menu not just to order but to check out what their competition at other fine restaurants were doing. While I may have been looking at an item's price on the menu, they were looking at the "pricing" on the menu. One of the gentlemen spoke of owning several fast food franchises, with one of them being in the Times Square district of New York. He spoke of the enormous real estate cost that he had to pay to own a business in that area and how he made it profitable. They strategized about partnerships that would create stronger businesses. They shared advice and information that would hopefully make their businesses grow. They spoke about how to make communities better through business ventures and community development. They discussed the stock market, hedge funds, life insurance, mutual funds, retirement, real estate, and politics. Most of it sounded like a foreign language to me. When they spoke about numbers, I would later find out that "five" or "ten" meant five million or ten million dollars. Mr. Boston would later find it amusing when I asked how they were buying businesses with five or ten dollars? I felt really dumb that night, but I sat there quietly because I wanted to become fluent in whatever language they were speaking. I learned that people with vision who may have started out working for McDonald's now *owned* them! I witnessed men bringing their business knowledge and wisdom together to share freely. As I ate, they talked, with some barely finishing their meal. It wasn't about the food for them, it was all about the conversations and exchange of information.

Once again, I found myself asking God, "Why am I here?" I then heard the words, "I have seated you in the company of great men so that you may learn and share what you are learning with people who may never have an opportunity like this." I would find myself in very similar settings after every seminar with Moneywise. My level of comfort would increase; however, I learned that during those times, my purpose in being there was to listen and absorb. I love conversing, but sometimes, it is our job to simply listen, so that we will have something meaningful to talk about later. I was motivated and inspired that night. I wanted to know more about business, wealth, and the people who were successful. I wrote down the names of every person at the table and Googled them when I got back to my hotel. These were men that I had never heard of before but were doing extremely well in life and business. They may not have all been multimillionaires, but they were all wealthy. With humility, they had all come together in Atlanta to hopefully motivate, educate, inspire, and empower people in the lower economic spectrum to aspire for higher places in life! These men were giving their time and knowledge to help others grow.

When was the last time that you were in a company of people who were where you aspired to be, but felt you had nothing to add to the conversation? When was the last time you sat there like a sponge, trying to absorb information that was way over your head? I challenge you to purposely place yourself in conversations and situations where you may not be the smartest cookie in the jar. Begin to position yourself in places and among people where you learn something new! Purposefully position yourself to sometimes be the least-informed in the group. Then, absorb information like a sponge. As a child, I used to hide under the table when my mother's relatives and friends gathered to eat, drink coffee, and talk. I heard a lot of things about life, good and bad, that as a little girl, went right over my head. However, now I have graduated from hiding under the table to sitting at the table. Some conversations still go over my head, but I now know that I am there to learn. Listening and learning from people who know more than you is essential to your growth.

Know more:

- _Purposely position yourself to be in the company of people who know way more than you do._
- _Feeling dumb simply means that there is more to learn._
- _Sometimes your purpose in the conversation is to be a sponge._

Lesson 13

THE MONEYWISE EXPERIENCE

"I stand in awe of You.

I can't believe all the promises have actually come true.

So, I stand in awe of You."

I met Mr. Kelvin Boston a couple of years before going on the Moneywise Empowerment Tour. The day my husband and I met this soft-spoken, bowtie-wearing gentleman, we had no idea of the impact he would have on our lives. When Mr. Boston approached my husband, who was also my manager, he stated that he was heading up a national financial empowerment tour. He wanted to know if I would be interested in joining as the featured singer. At this point, we still did not know who Mr. Boston was or what he actually did. So, I did what any other person would do in this age of technology; I Googled him! I discovered that Mr. Boston is the creator of "Moneywise with

Kelvin Boston," which is considered the Public Broadcasting System (PBS) network's premiere multicultural financial affairs program. The show has reached over 83 million households. Mr. Boston is also the author of *Who's Afraid to Be A Millionaire? – Mastering Financial and Emotional Success*, as well as the book *Smart Money Moves for African-Americans*. And now here I was, being offered the opportunity to join the Moneywise Empowerment Tour.

After viewing all his accomplishments, I must say that my husband and I were very impressed. So, following some questions, discussions, and prayer, we decided that I would join the tour. Part of my decision for joining the tour also came from my desire to help people who are in financial difficulty. This opportunity seemed like a great avenue for doing just that and it was not long before we were off and on our way. The first few seminars totally blew all my expectations out of the water! Mr. Boston calls it the "Moneywise Experience" and it certainly was an *experience*. Everything from videos to music to magic tricks were used as tools to get attendees excited about their financial potential. The speakers and presenters involved with the tour were men and women whom I had never heard of before. However, when they began to speak, their wealth of wisdom, knowledge, information, and inspiration was overwhelming! I

Googled every one of them and literally took pages and pages of notes from each speaker! Mr. Boston would often begin the tour by informing the attendees of his formula for success. He would state that "Time + Money + Opportunity = Success." All three are needed and all three require patience. He also instructed attendees to look at financial setbacks, such as job loss, losing a home, or even the recession, as a "new beginning" instead of the gloom and doom of a horrible ending. I would personally learn that my outlook on a financial situation determined my outcome. Mr. Boston firmly believes and teaches that to attain wealth, one must have a plan. Actually, not just *one* plan, but *three* plans. First, there must be a life plan. What are your dreams and how do you plan to achieve them? Secondly, there must be a financial plan. What are your financial goals? What steps are you taking to achieve them? Do you need a financial planner or a credit counselor? Lastly, he spoke of having a business plan. Mr. Boston teaches that the only way to true wealth and leaving a legacy behind is to own something. He is the entrepreneur guru of having your own business. He stresses the fact that ownership is power, and it helps insulate you during financially good and bad times. The information that I was personally receiving was like food to a starving stomach and water to one dying of thirst. My mind was feeding on information that it had never tasted before. When I was not singing, I was taking notes. For the first time in my life, I was not only being told that I *could* have financial freedom, but I was also being instructed *how* to accomplish it. Each speaker and panelist came to enlighten and inform. They all had one goal and that was to share their knowledge in the area of finances and wealth-building. Mr. Boston had amassed the best and brightest. And as I would later personally learn, they were also people of great character, conviction, and compassion.

It was a rare opportunity that the Moneywise team would travel to a city together. However, there were a few trips when Mr. Boston and I had the opportunity to travel together. At the time, my idea of a millionaire's lifestyle was shaped by what I had seen on television. Reality shows and other programs that showcased the lifestyles of the rich and famous had molded my knowledge of rich people and how they live. I envisioned the mansions, expensive cars, jewelry, designer clothing, private jets, and first-class travel. So, I was completely taken off-guard to see Mr. Boston standing in the same line as me, waiting to board the airplane with all the other passengers who were sitting in coach class! There was no entourage, flashy jewelry, or rolls of cash. His appearance was very inconspicuous. The car that he rented when we reached our destination was the least-expensive compact car and our hotel, although very nice, was booked through a budget travel website. His great humility in how he conducted himself and his money management was surprising, yet very refreshing. The restaurants we dined in were always excellent and some were absolutely amazing! I must say that I have had some of the best food in my life while on the road with the Moneywise Empowerment Tour. Dining out was the one area that made me feel like I was living the life of the rich and famous, as I had seen on television. What I would later learn is that great ideas, business deals, and important information were all shared over a great meal. Strong and powerful partnerships were also formed somewhere between the appetizers and dessert. There were times when we would occupy a table in a 5-star restaurant for hours. I would watch and listen to conversations, discussing everything from franchise opportunities to improving the financial situation of those communities hit hardest by the recession. Food was continually served, and glasses of fine wine flowed as freely as the conversation. The entire atmosphere intrigued and inspired me! I was now dining with men and women who owned casinos, hotels, food chain franchises, and other multimillion-dollar businesses. They walked with a grace and quiet power that allowed them to blend perfectly into the background. It was encounters like these that totally reshaped my beliefs on how wealthy people conduct themselves. I often felt like pinching myself in disbelief of the company that I was in.

I discovered that many enlightened people of wealth account for every dime as if it were their last. They are very aware that their money has purpose and is not meant to be wasted. I remember when Mr. Kenneth Brown, one of the speakers on the tour, was very upset because he had to change his flight at the last minute and it cost him an additional $300 to do so. With much compassion, he explained to me what happened. My thought at the time was: *$300 to you has to be like $3 to me. So why are you so upset?* He must have seen the expression on my face because he said, "Doreen, I just feel like I wasn't being a good steward over the money that God has blessed me with." His response of pure humility and gratitude for the wealth he had been blessed with took me completely by surprise. Although I had much less than this multimillionaire, it made me ask myself: *Am I being a good steward over what God has given me?*

Mr. Brown, who has one of the most amazing rags-to-riches stories that I have ever heard, also explained to me why he wears expensive, custom-made suits. He said, "Doreen, when I am announced as Ken Brown, motivational speaker and one of the youngest people to become a multimillionaire from McDonald's franchises, people are sizing me up within the first 30 seconds they see me. I only have one chance to make a first impression.

If my look does not match up to my introduction, then they may not listen to what I have to say." He went on to say that, "This suit is just a uniform. It is my work clothes. It's an investment in my business. I do not own dozens of them, only what I need." I later noticed that there were three-to-four suits consistently worn by the speakers and all were custom-made. Mr. Boston explained his custom-made suits by saying, "Because of the quality, they last for years. So, in the end, they are cost-effective." I did not know how much their suits cost, but I did know that when they suited up, they "suited up!" It did not matter if they wore signature bowties, like Mr. Kelvin Boston, or custom-made "speaker shoes", like Dr. Willie Jolley. When we met in the hotel lobby on Saturday mornings, they were dressed for the part and ready to go to work! Even their clothes had purpose. It made me wonder how many articles of clothing hung in my closet that had no purpose at all and were not even being worn. Although I was a bargain shopper, I was still being wasteful if I had a closet full of clothing that I never wore. This was definitely another "know more" moment for me. Again, I asked myself: *Am I being a good steward over the money that I have?*

Being the only woman traveling with the group, as well as a singer, I was not sure what my look should be. Should I wear business attire like the gentlemen or stay true to my look as a singer and entertainer? Although my clothing left few surprises to those on our tour, the hair was a whole different story! It would soon become a running joke, especially by our Human Resources Specialist, Mr. Carl Jefferson. He often would use me as an example during his presentations of what NOT to do with your hair. Mr. Jefferson would state that if you are working in corporate America, changing up your hairstyles drastically is not a good idea. He stated that it actually creates some trust issues in the workplace. He would then go on to say, "Unless you are Doreen Vail, Stellar Award-nominated recording artist, find a hairstyle and stick to it!" There would always be a lively discussion going on in the women's restroom during the break following his presentations. Some of the ladies got pretty heated, as I am sure some of you can imagine. Mr. Jefferson had no idea how close he came to needing a police escort to get out of the building at the end of the day. I never shared the story with him of getting stopped by security in the airport because of something that was detected in my carry-on luggage. I was pulled to the side along with my luggage and asked if I had something "organic" in my bag because it was detected during the screening. The security officer asked me the same question three times, with my answer consistently being "no", before he put on gloves and began to open my luggage. As he unzipped my carry-on suitcase, a clear plastic bag puffed up out of my luggage. He slowly began

111

to squeeze the plastic bag while inspecting it and then asked, "What is this?" And there she was, my afro wig and alter-ego, Sasha! Explaining my wig to this very nice, very young Caucasian airport security officer was quite an interesting and comical conversation. While walking to my gate, I thought to myself: *Carl was right. Hair can bring up trust issues.* I remember laughing until my plane landed at my destination.

Each and every presenter on the tour was a dynamic expert in their field! Mr. Robert Ferguson, creator and author of *Diet-Free for Life*, is the nutritionist and healthy living guru for the Moneywise Empowerment Tour. Mr. Boston believes that your greatest asset is your health, so it only made sense to have an expert like Robert Ferguson on the tour. Although he obviously practices what he preaches and is the picture of health, he never made others feel self-conscious about their food choices. Instead, while dining at fine restaurants and hotel breakfast buffets, he taught us how to eat what we wanted in a way that would not pack on the pounds. His approach is subtle and quite humorous. I would sit on the edge of my seat waiting for the point during his session when he would inform the audience to add butter to their baked potato. The people in the room would almost start to cheer! Like others in attendance, I felt that this was too good to be true. However, I can honestly say that Mr. Ferguson had no diet gimmicks that he was trying to push. He shared a great amount of information with the attendees, whether they purchased his book or not. He gives you the science and the facts behind living a healthy, diet-free life and his best client has been his mother, who has lost over 100 pounds! He is passionate about helping people live a healthier lifestyle, free from the restrictions of being on a never-ending diet. Mr. Ferguson taught me to find peace in being where I am currently and how to get where I want to be health-wise, all while enjoying the journey. We can have the best intentions and the greatest plans to have a wealthy life, but if we do not have our health, it's almost impossible to secure our wealth.

Another amazing speaker on the tour is Dr. Dennis Kimbro. He is a great educator and professor at the prestigious Clark University in Atlanta, Georgia. He is also the author of many books, including *Think and Grow Rich: A Black Choice*, *The Wealth Choice: Success Secrets of Black Millionaires*, and *What Makes the Great Great*, just to name a few. Dr. Kimbro is a phenomenal speaker and teacher! It does not matter if I am observing him speaking from a podium or around a dinner table, his passion to see everyone, especially those in poverty, reach their full potential is on fire. His presence fills the room, and his wisdom fills pages of notes. His booming voice demands your attention and his knowledge keeps it. Dr. Kimbro encourages us all to look within to extract the keys that underlie all accomplishments. He teaches sound principals about wealth. He states that the average individual gets at least four ideas a year that have the potential to make them wealthy if they truly acted on it. This makes me wonder. In my lifetime, how many wealth-creating ideas have I had and did nothing with? Dr. Kimbro also enlightens others on the hard work, sacrifices, and lifestyles of some of the multimillionaires that we admire. He has personally traveled the country interviewing scores of America's wealthiest and most notable African-American achievers. There are countless nuggets of gold that come from his mouth as he shares what he learned from the interviews. So much of what Dr. Kimbro teaches has given me many "know more" moments in my life. One that really stands out in particular is when he taught me that, "We are born with possibility and we live in fear." He stated that, "You must be afraid of losing your life and not accomplishing your dreams more than merely losing a house." I sat in the audience remembering the sleepless nights and all the anxiety that I felt as we fought so hard to keep our home. However, I could not say that I had ever placed as much effort in fighting to ensure that my dreams were accomplished. His words resonated greatly within me. They helped me overcome my fear as I strived to live my life by focusing on the great possibilities

114

that life had to offer. Dr. Kimbro is a man of great faith and compassion. He has taught me that there is a method to the madness of achieving wealth and that it is a method that anyone can learn. He also states that we may not all end up super-rich, but wealth is about much more than just money. I desperately needed that "know more" moment, since my definition of wealth had been defined only with a dollar sign followed by many numbers. I learned that wealth is also health, peace, empowerment, stability, and the ability to help others. All these things are achievable through learning and practicing wealthy ways. Another lesson that I have learned from Dr. Kimbro is not to chase money but to chase a fruitful life instead. He has also taught me to have great passion for what I am doing to help others. He has redefined what it means to truly be wealthy and helped me to understand that it's not merely a number. I have never met a more passionate man who loves his God, his family, and teaching people how to prosper more than Dr. Dennis Kimbro.

Mrs. Deborah Owens, another fantastic speaker on the tour, is a financial expert, author, and former financial executive. She is the founder and CEO of WEALTHYU and is known as "America's Wealth Coach." Mrs. Owens helps you look at your finances the way a physician looks at your health. They are either sick or well. She has a very unique coaching style, especially for women. Her desire to see a more leveled playing field for women and their finances is truly one of her passions. She is also the creator of *A Purse of Her Own*, a powerful tool for empowering women in their finances and practical methods for building wealth. I love her no-nonsense approach. Deborah Owens was the first to tell me that although I thought I was a very frugal shopper, I could still go broke shopping in the dollar store. She said that if I don't have the money to spend, it doesn't matter where I am shopping. That just makes too much sense and is such great advice! I also love how she explains the different levels of classes between the poor and the wealthy. She states, "The poor plan day-to-day. The middle class plans week-to-week. The rich plan year-to-year. The affluent plan decade-to-decade. The wealthy plan generation-to-generation." This revelation caused me to take a closer look at my spending habits, as well as my desire to leave a legacy of healthy finances and financial peace for my family. It was definitely a "know more" moment. Deborah Owens states that, "In the end, wealth is about giving and paying it forward to others." These are words I try to live by. The ability to give to and assist others who are less fortunate is my definition of enlightened wealth and power.

During one of our tours in the northeast, I was told that there would be a new motivational speaker joining us for that day. Once again, because of my limited knowledge on who's who, I had never heard the name Mrs. Gloria Mayfield Banks. However, I would soon be enlightened to the fact that she is the #1 ranked Elite National Sales Director for Mary Kay Cosmetics, annually leading her international sales team to multimillion-dollar success. When she entered the room, I felt that she needed her own theme music because her presence filled every inch of it. Her smile disarmed everyone, and her high energy left you looking for a seatbelt on your chair so you could buckle in. She was polished, glamorous, and beautiful, yet very down-to-earth. Her story about her climb to success from the overwhelming odds of dyslexia and living in an abusive marriage left us hanging on and inspired by her every word. There were no visible scars from what she had been through. Only elegance and grace exuded from her. She spoke from a place of grace and gratitude about her humble and difficult beginnings to her now very wealthy place in life. What I have gleaned from her is that money and wealth does not change what's already in the heart of a person. It just magnifies what is already there. Her heart is good. Her track record is in the thousands of women that she has inspired, motivated, and mentored into their own wealthy place. Although we only personally met on a couple of occasions, I still follow her closely on social media because she is such an inspiration to me! Gloria Mayfield Banks! I just love saying her entire name.

Now, if I am ever out on a ledge about to jump, I want you to call Dr. Willie Jolley to talk me down! He is another phenomenal speaker that I met on the tour. He can motivate and inspire anyone to want to live and never give up! Willie Jolley has been named one of the 5 most outstanding motivational speakers in the world! He is the author of the quote and book *A Setback is A Setup for A Comeback*, as well as a host of other motivational books and media. When he speaks, he captivates the audience from his first word to his last. He then takes the audience over the top with a song because he sings as well as he speaks. Dr. Jolley is a one-man show. My first time hearing him speak on the tour left me feeling like I could perhaps walk on water! During that seminar, he stated, "You must love people and use money, not love money and use people." He also stated, "God gave you the gift of life. Now what you do with it is your gift to God!" I never knew if Dr. Jolley was having a bad day because he motivated and inspired everyone from the ticket agents at the airport to the waiter or waitress at the restaurant. No one was a stranger to him and he taught me that every encounter is an opportunity to motivate and inspire someone. Dr. Jolley later became my mentor and my friend and even helped me greatly in writing this book. He firmly but wisely let me know that my first draft was not the book that I had intended to write and directed me to do it again. A hard pill to swallow, but like Mary Poppins, he has a way of putting your medicine in a spoonful of sugar to help it go down. The greatest "know more" lesson that I have learned from Willie Jolley is to never give up because my dreams are possible. He also helped me realize my value as a singer and a speaker. For him, with respect to achieving your goals, there's no such thing as "No," only "How?" He and his wife, Mrs. Dee Taylor-Jolley, form an extraordinary team in marriage and business. Watching them work the dream has encouraged my husband and me and let us know that dual partnerships in marriage and business can and do work.

The wealthy and enlightened people that I encountered are frugal. They understand that their money has *purpose*. They may live in homes that they have had for decades, although they may own multiple other investment properties. They are stable, like the multibillionaire Warren Buffett, who has lived in the same house since 1958. The wealthy men and women I have had the honor to meet often come from meager beginnings and they never forget where and how they started. The savvy ones do not tend to be big consumers. Instead, they are always brainstorming how to profit from the spending habits of others. They spend other people's money, while making their money grow into more money and power. They then take your money and invest it in their businesses, lives, and legacy. Just think, every time you spend a dollar, you are making someone else rich. In contrast, those who live paycheck-to-paycheck make money to spend money and spend until it's all gone. They then borrow money so that they may spend even more. It seems they are either paying bills for the items already purchased or making new bills. Many of us desire instant gratification from what we have worked all week to earn. However, this instant gratification comes at a great cost and often, the price that is paid is your peace of mind. All of us are the consumers that make rich people rich. The greatest lesson here is to understand that your money has *purpose* and there is a legacy in that purposeful money. Even if you are earning minimum wage, there are choices that you can make that will begin to bring financial balance and peace into your life. If you are mismanaging your money at the lowest level of income, it is likely that more money will only give you the opportunity to mismanage greater amounts of money.

Another important lesson that I learned from being a part of the Moneywise experience is that some enlightened millionaires will freely give you advice, but they will not easily part with their money. This was the most difficult lesson for me to initially understand. I was raised to give money to someone who says they needed it, especially if I have it. However, this is not the common practice for some of the enlightened wealthy people that I know. It is their desire to do more than simply "give a man a fish so that he may eat for a day." Their belief is that when you are continually addressing a person's financial needs through giving them money repeatedly, they will keep finding themselves in the same predicament; therefore, making them dependent on your handouts. For example, I often see a man in a wheelchair rolling himself down the white lines of the street in traffic asking for money. He is out there, day and night, rain or shine. Needless to say, many people, including myself, have rolled down our windows to give him a dollar or two. It is a very dangerous situation and I have seen some near-misses when he almost got hit and cars almost hitting each other while trying to avoid hitting him. One day, I thought to myself: *This is so dangerous for everyone. Why does he keep coming out here and risking his life and the lives of others?* It was then that I realized that our giving was actually keeping him in danger because he kept coming back for the money he received. Getting that "fish" every day had created a short-term daily fix, but what he needed was help for his long-term problems. He needed to be taught how to fish and build a lake that could supply his needs in a safe environment. What I have learned from the awesome company that I keep is

121

how to give in a way that will impact and change lives over the long-term and that knowledge is the key. Those committed to helping others change their lives and hopefully, the lives of generations to come, will not always give away a book to everyone who asks because they realize that there is value in someone making an investment in themselves. However, what these enlightened millionaires freely pass on is priceless knowledge, wisdom, and information that will teach the individual "how to fish" and create a stream that will take care of them and their generations to come! They want to empower others through knowledge. The great entertainer James Brown has a song lyric that says, *"I don't want nobody to give me nothing. Open up the door and I'll get it myself."* There is nothing like making and having your own money and creating your legacy instead of a dependency. There are some things that money definitely cannot buy, and wisdom and knowledge are two of them. If "what you don't know can't hurt you," then "what you *do* know can definitely help you!" I once read a quote by Mr. MacDonald of Def Jam Records, which said, *"People in high places will help you when you prove that you deserve it."*

The Moneywise Empowerment Tour has the capacity to literally change lives through the power of knowledge, motivation, and inspiration, just as it has changed my life. All that is required from the participants is an investment of their precious time. However, feelings of hopelessness are robbing so many people of the gift of time. They try many things to make that feeling of hopelessness surrounding their finances go away. Unfortunately, many of their choices are only making their financial matters worse and financial peace unobtainable. Wealth and financial peace take sacrifice, commitment, persistence, faith, diligence, a dream, hard work, and time. They also require a heart and mind that never gives up or takes no for an answer. I have found that many people want money, prosperity, and to escape the bondage of debt. However, they are not willing to put in the time, sacrifice, and labor necessary to achieve their goals. At the end of every single seminar, I hear the words, "I know so many people who needed to be here today to receive this information." The unfortunate reality is that the people who may need the information the most are not taking advantage of the opportunity. Hopelessness may be robbing them of the precious gift of time that could be spent being productive and impacting the lives of others. If this is you, I challenge you to gather your strength, dust off your dreams, and position yourself to increase in knowledge. You can say that you will be poor *no* more when you *know* more!

Every Moneywise seminar that I have experienced has left me stronger and wiser by the end of the day. There was so much that

I did not know. I also had so much incorrect thinking and misinformation in my head after years of trying to figure things out on my own. There were times that I had been given more information than I could process. So, I made a decision to focus on one-to-two things that I had learned from each seminar and earnestly attempt to put them into practice in my life. Although I don't always put into practice everything that I have learned, I have grown immensely in wisdom surrounding my finances. It's been several years and scores of seminars since joining the Moneywise Empowerment Tour founded by Mr. Kelvin Boston. To this day, I still leave each seminar more informed and as excited than I was the first time. The speakers and panelists never cease to inform, amaze, and teach me. The wisdom and knowledge seem endless. The passion and compassion in their desire to educate people to achieve a better financial way of life is felt with every word. Moneywise is an experience that changes lives. The exposure has taught me how a wealthy mindset thinks and what they know that the average person doesn't. I have been able to say "No more" to so many of the bad habits and "stinking thinking" that robbed me of discovering financial peace. Thank you, Mr. Boston, for the opportunity to help myself and others. I thank the entire team for helping me build my lake.

Know more:

- _Fear will stifle possibility in your life._
- _Being moneywise is a daily commitment._
- _Wisdom is realizing you need more knowledge._
- _Your money and wealth have purpose._
- _Your health and your time are your most priceless commodities._
- _To continue a plan that is not working is insanity._
- _The best information is information that helps you obtain the insight to resolve your own financial challenges._
- _Never pack your human hair wig in your carry-on luggage._

Lesson 14

JOURNEY TO FINANCIAL PEACE

"The Lord is my Shepard. I lack nothing."

– Psalm 23:1

I have purchased a ticket to ride this rollercoaster more times than I can remember. After riding the highs and lows, the twists and turns, I returned to the gate again and again for the same scary experience. My journey to financial peace began much like the slow ascent of a rickety rollercoaster ride. What started out as one credit card approval on the tracks of this rollercoaster ride slowly heightened to being fully-loaded with more debt than I could manage by the time my financial ride reached top-speed. From getting my first paycheck as a teenager, to my first credit card and student loan as a college student, to acquiring new furniture and cars as a young wife, to medical bills as a new mother, the time spent at the top of my finances seemed like seconds in my life before spiraling down into the rapid decline. There were times when the ride moved so fast that it literally took my sleep, hope, peace, and literal breath away! I felt at times that I needed to be hooked up to oxygen just to breathe. The phone calls from creditors that filled my answering machine to capacity and the white envelopes stamped "FINAL NOTICE" that covered my dining room table robbed me of my peace and almost my sanity. I prayed, I cried, and I worried. I had sleepless nights and stressful days. I didn't answer my phone and I didn't open the mail. While spiraling down on this financial rollercoaster ride, it was all I could do some days just to hold on and tighten my grip. I couldn't get off and I couldn't let go. Dying wasn't an option but it was a thought. Knowing that at some point, this ride would have to come to an end was all that there was to hold on to some days.

This journey to financial peace has had many twists and turns and many ups and downs. There were many times when hopelessness was the soup of the day and I ate more than my fair share. Because of my faith in God, giving up was never an option. Although I may not have received immediate relief, I always knew that my prayers were being heard and would eventually be answered. It was what I learned and did during that waiting period that would make me stronger and better. I realized that if

I was to get a prayer answered, I would have to be an active participant once I finished praying. I learned that since I played a very active role in getting myself into the financial situation, I would have to play a very active role in getting myself out. Although the descent was rapid, the ascent would once again be a slow and tedious ride, one click on the tracks at a time. So, with every step, my endurance increased. With every bill that was paid on time, my credit score went up a few points. With every penny saved, breathing became a little easier. With every prayer, my faith became a little stronger. While sharing my story to help others, my hope was restored. I replaced recklessness with self-control, and pity with patience. I learned what not to do from the bumps in this financial road. However, sometimes, I still trip over them. I forgave myself and promised myself I would do better. I no longer live in fear, but I walk by faith. I know that even with the best financial planning, anything can happen at any time that could send me plummeting down the rollercoaster ride once again. But my journey has taught me never to lose hope.

There is an old saying that says, "I wouldn't trade anything for my journey now," and that is the statement that best fits my journey to financial peace. I have discovered that for me, the definition of wealth is not measured in numbers and dollar signs. It is measured in the ability to have a house that is a home for my family and me. It is measured by my ability to have all I need and still be able to help meet the needs of others. It is measured by how many times I laugh and smile in a day and how many times I can make others do the same. My wealth is measured by how well I can live within my means while I strive to always have more than what I need. It is the ability to enjoy the things in life and see as much of this amazing world as I can. It doesn't matter if I am in the front or the back of the plane; we all arrive at the same place at the same time. It is the ability to give and help others without worrying about lacking what my family and I need. Wealth is the ability to share. Wealth is *peace* to me. Pure, priceless *peace.* Strive to define and find *your* wealthy place. I can assure you that it can be found by knowing more about how enlightened, wealthy people think and live. You can say no to being poor by knowing more. Blessings on your journey to financial peace! You can do this!

Know more:

- *Wealth is understanding that your life has a value that no number can define.*

- *Define wealth by the financial peace that it brings.*

- *Your wealthy place is found between what you want and what you need.*

- *When times get tough, the tough get laughing.*

BIOGRAPHY

Doreen Vail is "therapy." Her music, songs, words, storytelling, smile, and presence all have a therapeutic effect on others. She is a national and international songstress, speaker, storyteller, and now an author. During your first introduction to Doreen, you will notice her signature smile, which is bright and contagious. While working as an Occupational Therapy Assistant, she was nicknamed "The Songbird" by hospital patients and staff. When she opens her mouth to sing or to speak, you just *feel* it!

Doreen was born and raised in New York. She grew up in Hempstead, Long Island with her parents and four siblings. She moved to North Carolina as a teenager, where she met and married her high-school sweetheart, Seth Vail. They are the proud parents of two beautiful daughters, Crystale and Taryn. They are also the proud grandparents of five amazing grandchildren. She has worked as a licensed Occupational

Therapy Assistant for over 25 years in various healthcare facilities and loves her profession. She is also a humanitarian, donating her time and resources to children, homeless shelters, nursing homes, prisons, and mission trips abroad. People are her passion.

Singing has been as natural for Doreen as breathing. Her powerful vocals have been compared to those of other great vocalists. However, most people agree that she has a unique style that is all her own. Doreen is a 2009 Stellar Award nominee for "Contemporary Female Artist of the Year" for her sophomore project, entitled *Odyssey*. Doreen's first CD, **Reflections of a Yielded Vessel**, opened international doors through worldwide television, radio, and internet exposure. She presently tours nationally with the prestigious Moneywise Empowerment Tour, where she is a featured inspirational and motivational singer and speaker. Doreen also co-produced the season 4 version of the theme song "Way Down in the Hole" for the highly-acclaimed HBO series **"The Wire."** She realizes that her greatest assets are her voice and her heart. When the two collide, no matter what the platform, God uses her to impact lives in a therapeutic way! Doreen just has a way of making people feel better.

Made in the USA
Middletown, DE
16 April 2018